Salad

THE AUSTRALIAN
Women's Weekly

Salad

contents

introduction

With the great variety of salad leaves now available, it's no wonder salads have become the stars of modern cuisine. Salad is wonderfully versatile – it can be served as a starter, side dish, an impressive main meal, and a refreshing dessert. Salads offer a variety of textures, colours and flavours to a meal, and are an easy way to ensure we get those all-important five servings of vegies each day.

The popularity of salads is evident from the increasing number of salad bars and the availability of ready-to-use salad stuffs in supermarkets. And the greater availability of fresh and exotic ingredients has meant that our salads have become more interesting and enticing.

The leaves used for salads can range from iceberg, cos, chicory, radicchio, mignonette, witlof, watercress to baby spinach leaves. It is essential to select well when you buy. The golden rule is to purchase in season, when they are at their peak and, therefore, less expensive. Thoroughly wash all your salad leaves, whether they have been pre-washed or not. Dry well, preferably in a salad spinner, but a clean tea towel will also do the trick.

Colour, flavour and crunch can be added with vegetables like capsicum, corn, red onion and asparagus. Avocado, with its rich buttery flesh, is the perfect partner for a salad containing seafood, such as prawns, salmon or lobster. Pecans, walnuts, almonds or pine nuts, roasted in the oven or frying pan, provide a delicious crunch when sprinkled on top of a salad, or try the Soy salad seed mix on page 7.

Salad tips

Storage

Store lettuce and salad leaves in the crisper of your refrigerator in order to keep them fresh. Herbs should be kept standing upright in a glass or jug half-filled with water and covered with a plastic bag. Alternatively line an airtight plastic container with a paper towel, lay the herbs on top, cover with another dry paper towel and seal the lid, then store in the fridge. Tomatoes and avocados should always be kept at room temperature until fully ripe, as they will not ripen after chilling.

Dressings

Dressings can vary from a simple vinaigrette to the rich and creamy. Different kinds of salads require different dressings – a simple vinaigrette is best on a complicated salad; a sharp vinegary dressing is good on tomato salads; a creamy dressing is lovely on crisp or soft salad leaves. For a different twist use lemon juice instead of vinegar or try avocado instead of mayo in creamy dressings.

How to dress a salad

Avoid overdressing salads as this can drown out the other flavours. Almost all of us make more dressing than we need. Just before serving, pour on about half as much dressing as you think you'll need and toss the salad. You can always add a little more but too much dressing and you'll end up with a puddle at the bottom of the bowl and a very soggy salad.

Cooking vegetables for salads

There are some vegetables that go particularly well in salads: snow peas, sugar snap peas, asparagus, broccolini, and beans. They should be blanched, or very lightly boiled, steamed or cooked in the microwave until still crisp – never ever mushy. Immediately drain your vegies and refresh with cold water to prevent any further cooking and to retain their bright colour. Dry well before adding to your salad. Roasted vegetables make wonderful warm salads: sweet potato, pumpkin, potato and beetroot are delicious teamed with fetta or goats cheese. Beetroot, either roasted or canned, should always be added at the last minute. Its rich beautiful colour doesn't look so striking when is has bled through the salad and turned everything pink.

Salad seed mixtures

You can buy salad seed mixtures at some greengrocers and supermarkets but it's easy to make your own (and cheaper too). Sprinkle them over salads or steamed or baked vegetables.

Soy salad seed mix

100g sesame seeds
100g sunflower seeds
100g pepitas
40g pine nuts
1 tablespoon soy sauce

Dry-fry seeds and pine nuts in medium frying pan over medium heat, taking care not to allow them to burn, stirring constantly until the sesame seeds start to pop and the rest of the ingredients toast slightly. Place immediately in a bowl then stir in soy sauce while seed mixture is hot. Store in an airtight container in the fridge.

oils

1 Olive oil

The juice extracted from fresh olives. Extra virgin olive oil is the oil extracted from the first cold pressing and contains the most health benefits. Extra virgin olive oil can range in flavour from mild and fruity to robust and peppery.

'Pure', 'light' and 'extra light' olive oils have been refined and they lack the aroma, flavour and the natural antioxidant content of extra virgin olive oil. In fact the word "light" refers only to their light colour, aroma and flavour, not to fat content. All olive oils have the same fat content.

Price is usually a guide to quality. Buy olive oil in small quantities – it becomes rancid over time – and store in a cool, dark place.

2 Peanut oil

Pressed from ground peanuts. It is most commonly used in Asian cooking because of its high smoke point – the capacity to handle high heat without burning.

3 Vegetable oil

Any of a number of oils sourced from plant rather than animal fats; it is flavourless and odourless so ideal when you need a bland oil.

4 Sesame oil

Made from roasted, crushed, white sesame seeds. Has a very strong flavour and is used sparingly, more as a flavouring than a cooking medium.

5 Walnut oil, hazelnut oil, macadamia oil

All have a distinctive nutty flavour. They are used in dressings and sauces, and can add a lovely nutty quality to baking.

1 Balsamic vinegar

Very distinctive Italian vinegar; there are now many balsamic vinegars on the market, ranging in pungency and quality depending on how, and for how long, they have been aged. The rich, sweet, and complex flavour becomes more mellow and sweet with age. It is used in salad dressings and is especially good when teamed with the pepperiness of rocket. We use supermarket-quality balsamic in our recipes. If using an expensive, aged imported vinegar, use it in smaller quantities than we suggest in our recipes. For example, use 1 teaspoon of excellent quality balsamic instead of 1 tablespoon of supermarket-quality balsamic.

2 White balsamic vinegar

Made from white wine vinegar; the flavour is almost identical to regular balsamic vinegar; recipes usually include it (instead of regular balsamic vinegar) for aesthetic reasons, so as not to colour sauces or dressings.

3 Cider vinegar

Also known as apple cider vinegar; made from fermented apples and has a brownish-yellow colour. It has a distinctive sweet apple flavour and goes particularly well in relishes, dressings and pork dishes.

4 White wine vinegar, red wine vinegar

Made respectively from white wine and red wine. As with wine, there is a considerable range in quality. Both are commonly used in salad dressings. Both give a more mellow rounded flavour than white or malt vinegar.

5 Malt vinegar

A classic condiment for fish and chips; it is traditionally made from unhopped beer and has a strong flavour that is good for robust-flavoured dressings, pickles and relishes.

6 Rice vinegar, rice wine vinegar

Made from fermented rice and flavoured with sugar and salt. Its delicate flavour makes it very versatile; it is used in the preparation of sushi rice, is lovely in salad dressings and is often used in asian dipping sauces.

7 Sherry vinegar

Natural vinegar aged in oak according to the traditional Spanish system; a mellow wine vinegar, sweeter than red or white wine vinegar, and named for its colour. It is beautiful in a vinaigrette and is excellent when used for deglazing roasting and frying pans when making a sauce.

vinegars

mustards

1 Flat-leaf parsley
Often referred to as 'italian' or 'continental parley', it is stronger in flavour and darker in colour than curly parsley.

2 Oregano
Particularly prominent in Italian and Greek cuisines, it is often used with grilled meat, in tomato sauce, soup and on pizzas.

3 Mint
Often used with lamb, potatoes, peas and in fruit salads, and the sprigs are used in drinks and to make a simple tea. There are many varieties available.

4 Vietnamese mint
Identified mainly with Vietnamese cuisine, it is stronger in flavour and more peppery than regular mint and is commonly used fresh in salads and in rice paper rolls.

1 English, hot english
Traditional hot, pungent, deep-yellow mustard. Serve with roast beef and ham; wonderful with hard cheeses.

2 Wholegrain, honey wholegrain
A french-style, coarse grain mustard made from crushed mustard seeds and dijon-style french mustard. Works well with cold meats and sausages.

3 Dijon, honey dijon
French in origin, pale brown and creamy with a fairly mild flavour. Delicious in salad dressings, especially for potato salad, and on meat.

4 American
Bright yellow in colour, a sweet mustard containing mustard seeds, sugar, salt, spices and garlic. Serve with hot dogs and hamburgers.

5 Basil

Also known as sweet basil, it is particularly popular in Italian dishes and the main ingredient of pesto; used with tomatoes.

6 Thai basil

One of the identifying flavours of Thai food, it has a slight aniseed taste. The leaves are smaller than sweet basil and the stems are purple.

7 Coriander

Also known as cilantro, it is used in a wide variety of cuisines, from Latin American to South-East Asian. The seeds, leaves, stem and roots can all be used and they each have a different flavour; it has a pungent aroma and taste and is a must in Thai green curry. Dried coriander seeds cannot be used as a substitute.

8 Tarragon

An essential flavour in many classic French dishes, it has a strong aniseed flavour. Be sure to use the french variety, not russian, as the russian is not nearly as aromatic and flavoursome as its french counterpart.

9 Chives

Related to the onion and leek, it has a subtle onion flavour and is often used with eggs, in salads or as a garnish.

10 Thyme, lemon thyme

A member of the mint family, the strong aromatic leaves are very versatile and are often used in soups, meat dishes, particularly terrines and pâtés, and are a lovely alternative to rosemary on roast potatoes. Lemon thyme has a strong citrus aroma and flavour.

11 Dill

The distinctly feathery, frond-like leaves have an aniseed/celery sweetness and are good with potato salad and fish.

12 Rosemary

Sprig of long, thin pointy leaves with a strong pungent flavour, it is particularly good on roast potatoes and with lamb.

13 Chervil

Mild fennel-flavoured member of the parsley family; a staple in French cuisine and is often used in omelettes, salads and soups.

herbs

1 Iceberg lettuce

Heavy, firm round lettuce with tightly packed leaves and crisp texture.

2 Cos lettuce, baby cos lettuce

Elongated in shape with leaves ranging from dark green on the outside to almost white near the core; the traditional caesar salad lettuce.

3 Butter lettuce

Round, loosely formed head with a sweet flavour and soft, pale green leaves.

4 Mesclun

Commercial blend of green salad leaves, including baby spinach leaves, mizuna and curly endive.

5 Oak leaf lettuce

Soft, curly-leafed lettuce found in both green and red varieties.

6 Rocket, baby rocket, wild rocket

Also known as arugula or rucola, it is a peppery green leaf eaten raw in salads or wilted in rice and pasta dishes. Baby rocket leaves are smaller and less peppery; wild rocket leaves are firmer with a richer, nuttier taste.

7 Radicchio

Italian in origin, this lettuce brings a deep purple colour and a distinctive bitter flavour to salads. It can also be cooked, usually grilled or tossed through hot pasta until just wilted. It does lose its crimson colour when heated, but will develop a sweet, mellow flavour.

8 Baby spinach leaves

Small, bright green leaves that are best eaten raw in salads or cooked until barely wilted.

9 Red coral lettuce

Very curly and tightly furled red leaves that resemble coral and have a mild, sweet taste.

10 Mizuna, baby mizuna

A Japanese green with serrated, dark green leaves with narrow white stalks and a mild peppery flavour; often found in mesclun. Baby mizuna are lighter and have a milder flavour. Mizuna is most commonly used fresh in salads or added to soups and stir-fries.

11 Tat soi, baby tat soi

A Chinese green with dark green spoon-shaped leaves and distinctive long, white stalks; has a soft creamy texture and a subtle flavour. Baby tat soi is smaller and lighter in colour.

salad leaves

12 White witlof, red witlof, baby witlof

Witlof, meaning "white leaf" in Dutch; also known as belgian endive; narrow, elongated bulbous clusters of leaves that are creamy white to light yellow in colour and slightly bitter in flavour; the whiter the leaf, the less bitter the taste. Red varieties are also available, as well as baby witlof which is slightly less bitter. All can be eaten fresh, either chopped in salads or whole, or cooked. The flavour mellows and becomes less bitter with cooking.

13 Endive, curly endive

Related to chicory, endive has broad, pale green leaves and a slightly bitter flavour. Curly endive, also known as frisée, has a fairly bitter flavour with narrow and prickly looking curly outer leaves and an edible white heart.

14 Savoy cabbage

Heavy round head with tightly packed light green, crinkly leaves. It has a mild, sweet flavour.

15 Red cabbage

Deep purple in colour, the inner leaves are tightly packed while the outer leaves are softer and more loosely attached and resemble a flower. It is often braised, pickled or shredded and eaten raw in salads.

16 Watercress

Deep green, clover-shaped leaves that have a peppery, spicy flavour. It is most commonly used in salads or made into a delightful soup.

17 Lamb's lettuce

Also known as corn salad, it has round or spoon shaped velvety green leaves with a mild nutty flavour. It is usually used in salads but can also be cooked until just wilted.

18 Snow pea tendrils

The thin, delicately crisp new growth of the snow pea plant, including the tender uppermost leaves and the tendrils that enable the plant to climb. These delicious tendrils are full of pea flavour and are often used as a garnish. If you can't find them, use snow pea sprouts instead.

19 Snow pea sprouts

Thin, light-green shoots and leaves with a smooth white to light green stalk; they have a delicate, sweet flavour and can be eaten raw, used in soups, steamed, or stir-fried.

20 Bean sprouts

Tender new growths of assorted beans and seeds. The most readily available are mung bean, soybean and alfalfa sprouts. They are often used in salads, stir-fries or sandwiches.

classic salads

tabbouleh, page 18

No matter how much we love new and innovative salads, we keeping coming back to the classics. There are some salads, such as tabbouleh, Greek salad and Caesar salad that simply can't be improved on.

tabbouleh

¼ cup (40g) burghul
3 medium tomatoes (450g)
3 cups coarsely chopped fresh flat-leaf parsley
3 green onions, chopped finely
½ cup coarsely chopped fresh mint
1 clove garlic, crushed
¼ cup (60ml) lemon juice
¼ cup (60ml) olive oil

1 Place burghul in shallow medium bowl. Halve tomatoes, scoop pulp from tomato over burghul. Chop tomato flesh finely; spread over burghul. Cover; refrigerate 1 hour.

2 Place burghul mixture in large bowl with remaining ingredients; stir to combine.

prep time *30 minutes (+ refrigeration)* serves *4*
nutritional count per serving *14.2g total fat
(2g saturated fat); 790kJ (189 cal); 9.4g carbohydrate;
3.6g protein; 5.9g fibre*

Perfect tabbouleh relies on perfect parsley: it's imperative that the parsley is well washed to remove any grit and dried thoroughly before adding to the salad. If the parsley is too wet, you will find that your tabbouleh turns a little mushy, rather than being light and tasty.

chef's salad

4 rindless bacon rashers (260g)
1 iceberg lettuce, leaves separated, torn
150g thinly sliced leg ham, chopped coarsely
150g roasted turkey breast, shredded
3 medium tomatoes (450g), chopped coarsely
3 radishes (105g), trimmed, sliced thinly
150g roquefort cheese, crumbled
1 large avocado (320g), sliced thinly

roquefort dressing
1 tablespoon dijon mustard
¼ cup (60ml) white wine vinegar
50g roquefort cheese, crumbled
½ cup (125ml) extra-virgin olive oil

1 Make roquefort dressing.

2 Cook bacon in large oiled frying pan until crisp; chop coarsely.

3 Place lettuce in large serving bowl with remaining salad ingredients. Drizzle with dressing; toss gently to combine.

roquefort dressing Combine mustard, vinegar and cheese in small bowl. Gradually whisk in the oil until the mixture becomes thick.

prep & cook time *30 minutes* serves *6*
nutritional count per serving *41.3g total fat (12.2g saturated
fat); 2107J (504 cal); 2.2g carbohydrate; 30.8g protein;
2.6g fibre*

chef's salad

caesar salad

Named after Caesar Cardini, the Italian-American who tossed the first caesar salad in Mexico during the 1920s, this salad always contains fresh croûtons, crisp cos lettuce leaves, lightly boiled eggs, lemon juice, olive oil, worcestershire and parmesan but no one ingredient should dominate.

½ loaf ciabatta (220g)
1 clove garlic, crushed
⅓ cup (80ml) olive oil
2 eggs
3 baby cos lettuces, trimmed, leaves separated
1 cup (80g) flaked parmesan cheese

caesar dressing
1 clove garlic, crushed
1 tablespoon dijon mustard
2 tablespoons lemon juice
2 teaspoons worcestershire sauce
2 tablespoons olive oil

1 Preheat oven to 180°C/160°C fan-forced.

2 Cut bread into 2cm cubes; combine garlic and oil in large bowl with bread. Toast bread on oven tray until croûtons are browned.

3 Place ingredients for caesar dressing in screw-top jar; shake well.

4 Bring water to the boil in small saucepan, add eggs; cover pan tightly, remove from heat. Remove eggs from water after 2 minutes. When cool enough to handle, break eggs into large bowl; add lettuce, mixing gently so egg coats leaves.

5 Add cheese, croûtons and dressing to bowl; toss gently to combine.

prep & cook time *45 minutes* serves *4*
nutritional count per serving *39.1g total fat (9.1g saturated fat); 2366kJ (566 cal); 33.1g carbohydrate; 18.4g protein; 5.6g fibre*

salade composé

Literally meaning "composed salad", the ingredients in this dish are layered on top of each other, rather than being tossed together, and the dressing is drizzled over the top.

1 small french bread stick (150g)
2 cloves garlic, crushed
¼ cup (60ml) olive oil
6 rindless bacon rashers (390g), sliced thickly
150g mesclun
6 medium egg tomatoes (450g), sliced thinly
4 hard-boiled eggs, halved lengthways

red wine vinaigrette
¼ cup (60ml) red wine vinegar
3 teaspoons dijon mustard
⅓ cup (80ml) extra virgin olive oil

1 Preheat grill.

2 Cut bread into 1cm slices. Brush both sides with combined garlic and oil; toast under preheated grill.

3 Cook bacon in large frying pan until crisp; drain on absorbent paper.

4 Meanwhile, place ingredients for red wine vinaigrette in screw-top jar; shake well.

5 Layer bread and bacon in large bowl with mesclun and tomato, top with egg; drizzle with vinaigrette.

prep & cook time *35 minutes* serves *4*
nutritional count per serving *51.8g total fat (11.1g saturated fat); 2859kJ (684 cal); 23.4g carbohydrate; 30.5g protein; 3.9g fibre*

caesar salad

salade composé

waldorf salad

4 medium red apples (600g)
¼ cup (60ml) lemon juice
5 stalks celery (750g), trimmed, chopped coarsely
1 cup (110g) coarsely chopped roasted walnuts
1 cup (300g) mayonnaise (see page 331)

1 Core unpeeled apples; cut into thin wedges.

2 Place apple in large serving bowl with remaining ingredients; toss gently to combine.

prep time *15 minutes* serves *4*
nutritional count per serving *63.1g total fat (7.8g saturated fat); 2800kJ (670 cal); 17.8g carbohydrate; 6.8g protein; 6.5g fibre*

A signature dish from the kitchen of New York's world-famous Waldorf-Astoria hotel, the waldorf salad was created at the beginning of the 20th century, and proved so popular that it rapidly became a staple in kitchens throughout America.

caprese salad

3 large egg tomatoes (270g), sliced thinly
300g bocconcini cheese, drained, sliced thinly
2 tablespoons olive oil
¼ cup firmly packed fresh basil leaves, torn

1 Overlap slices of tomato and cheese on serving platter.

2 Drizzle with oil; sprinkle with basil.

prep time *15 minutes* serves *4*
nutritional count per serving *20.6g total fat (8.8g saturated fat); 1028kJ (246 cal); 1.6g carbohydrate; 13.6g protein; 1.1g fibre*

panzanella

1 litre (4 cups) water
250g stale sourdough bread, cut into 2cm slices
2 large tomatoes (440g), chopped coarsely
1 small red onion (100g), sliced thinly
2 lebanese cucumbers (260g), chopped coarsely
1 cup firmly packed fresh basil leaves
2 tablespoons olive oil
2 tablespoons red wine vinegar
1 clove garlic, crushed

1 Place the water in large shallow bowl; briefly dip bread slices into water. Pat dry with absorbent paper; tear bread into large chunks.

2 Place bread in large bowl with remaining ingredients; toss gently to combine.

prep time *20 minutes* serves *4*
nutritional count per serving *11g total fat (1.5g saturated fat); 1104kJ (264 cal); 33.2g carbohydrate; 7.5g protein; 6g fibre*

greek salad

4 medium egg tomatoes (300g), sliced thinly
2 lebanese cucumbers (260g), chopped coarsely
1 small red onion (100g), sliced thinly
½ cup (75g) seeded kalamata olives
150g fetta cheese, chopped coarsely
2 tablespoons olive oil
2 tablespoons lemon juice
2 teaspoons fresh oregano leaves

1 Combine tomato, cucumber, onion, olives and cheese in large bowl.

2 Place remaining ingredients in screw-top jar; shake well. Drizzle dressing over salad.

prep time *15 minutes* serves *4*
nutritional count per serving *18.2g total fat (7.1g saturated fat); 991kJ (237 cal); 9g carbohydrate; 8.3g protein; 2.4g fibre*

oak leaf salad

1 green oak leaf lettuce, leaves separated
¼ cup coarsely chopped fresh chives
½ cup firmly packed fresh flat-leaf parsley leaves
½ cup firmly packed fresh chervil leaves

dijon vinaigrette
2 tablespoons olive oil
2 tablespoons white wine vinegar
1 tablespoon dijon mustard
2 teaspoons white sugar

1 Place ingredients for dijon vinaigrette in screw-top jar; shake well.

2 Place salad ingredients in medium bowl with dressing; toss gently to combine.

prep time *10 minutes* serves *6*
nutritional count per serving *6.2g total fat (0.9g saturated fat); 288kJ (69 cal); 2g carbohydrate; 0.7g protein; 1.1g fibre*

caprese salad

greek salad

panzanella

oak leaf salad

fattoush

6 pocket pitta (500g)
olive oil, for shallow-frying
3 medium tomatoes (450g), chopped coarsely
1 large green capsicum (350g), chopped coarsely
2 lebanese cucumbers (260g), seeded, sliced thinly
10 trimmed red radishes (150g), sliced thinly
4 spring onions (100g), sliced thinly
1½ cups firmly packed fresh flat-leaf parsley leaves
½ cup coarsely chopped fresh mint

lemon garlic dressing
2 cloves garlic, crushed
¼ cup (60ml) olive oil
¼ cup (60ml) lemon juice

1 Halve pitta horizontally; cut into 2.5cm pieces. Heat oil in wok or large frying pan; shallow-fry pitta, in batches, until browned lightly and crisp. Drain on absorbent paper.

2 Place ingredients for lemon garlic dressing in screw-top jar; shake well.

3 Just before serving, place about three-quarters of the pitta in large bowl with dressing and remaining ingredients; toss gently to combine. Sprinkle remaining pitta over fattoush.

prep & cook time *35 minutes* serves *4*
nutritional count per serving *30.5g total fat (4.2g saturated fat); 2688kJ (643 cal); 72.5g carbohydrate; 15.4g protein; 8.4g fibre*

coleslaw

½ small cabbage (600g), shredded finely
1 medium carrot (120g), grated coarsely
4 green onions, sliced thinly
½ cup (150g) mayonnaise
1 tablespoon lemon juice

1 Combine ingredients in large bowl.

prep time *10 minutes* serves *6*
nutritional count per serving *8.1g total fat (1g saturated fat); 523kJ (125 cal); 8.8g carbohydrate; 2g protein; 4.5g fibre*

potato salad

2kg potatoes, peeled
2 tablespoons cider vinegar
4 green onions, sliced thinly
¼ cup finely chopped fresh flat-leaf parsley
1 cup (300g) mayonnaise (see page 331)

1 Cover potatoes with cold water in large saucepan; bring to the boil. Reduce heat; simmer, covered, until tender. Drain; cut into 3cm pieces. Spread potato on a tray, sprinkle with vinegar; refrigerate until cold.

2 Place potato in large bowl with mayonnaise, onion and parsley; toss gently to combine.

prep & cook time *45 minutes (+ refrigeration)*
nutritional count per serving *30.4g total fat (4.1g saturated fat); 1764kJ (422 cal); 29g carbohydrate; 6.2g protein; 3.7g fibre*

Properly cooked, any waxy, white-fleshed potato will hold its shape when tossed in a salad.

coleslaw

potato salad

coronation chicken

1½ cups (300g) basmati rice
700g chicken breast fillets
1 cup (300g) mayonnaise (see page 331)
½ cup (120g) sour cream
1 teaspoon curry powder
2 cups loosely packed fresh basil leaves
5 ripe nectarines (850g), cut into wedges
2 cups (300g) roasted unsalted cashews

1 Cook rice in large saucepan of boiling water, uncovered, until tender; drain. Rinse under cold water; drain.

2 Meanwhile, poach chicken, covered, in large frying pan of boiling water about 10 minutes or until cooked through. Cool chicken in liquid 10 minutes; slice thinly.

3 Combine mayonnaise, cream and curry powder in large bowl. Add chicken, basil, nectarine and three-quarters of the nuts; toss gently to combine.

4 Divide rice among serving plates; top with chicken mixture, sprinkle with remaining nuts.

prep & cook time *45 minutes* serves *6*
nutritional count per serving *55.6g total fat (13.5g saturated fat); 3946kJ (944 cal); 68.6g carbohydrate; 39.6g protein; 7.2g fibre*

This is our contemporary take on the salad invented by renowned British cook Constance Spry, for the 1953 coronation of Queen Elizabeth II.

salade niçoise

The original French salade niçoise was created with the finest local produce from Provence – vine-ripened tomatoes, piquant caperberries, tiny, firm black olives, hand-picked baby beans and good-quality canned tuna. Our version has adapted a modern approach more suitable to our hectic lifestyle.

200g baby green beans, trimmed
2 tablespoons olive oil
1 tablespoon lemon juice
2 tablespoons white wine vinegar
4 medium tomatoes (600g), cut into wedges
4 hard-boiled eggs, quartered
425g can tuna in springwater, drained, flaked
½ cup (80g) drained caperberries, rinsed
½ cup (60g) seeded small black olives
¼ cup firmly packed fresh flat-leaf parsley leaves
440g can drained whole new potatoes, rinsed, halved

1   Boil, steam or microwave beans until tender; drain. Rinse under cold water; drain.

2   Whisk oil, juice and vinegar in large bowl; add beans and remaining ingredients, mix gently.

prep & cook time *20 minutes*   serves *4*
nutritional count per serving *16.9g total fat (3.7g saturated fat); 1522kJ (364 cal); 19.5g carbohydrate; 30.9g protein; 5.2g fibre*

pasta salad

250g orecchiette pasta
2 tablespoons drained sun-dried tomatoes, chopped coarsely
1 small red onion (100g), sliced thinly
1 small green capsicum (150g), sliced thinly
½ cup coarsely chopped fresh flat-leaf parsley

sun-dried tomato dressing
1 tablespoon sun-dried tomato pesto
2 tablespoons olive oil
1 tablespoon white wine vinegar

1   Cook pasta in large saucepan of boiling water, uncovered, until just tender; drain. Rinse under cold water; drain.

2   Place ingredients for sun-dried tomato dressing in screw-top jar; shake well.

3   Place pasta in large bowl with remaining ingredients and dressing; toss gently to combine.

prep & cook time *25 minutes*   serves *4*
nutritional count per serving *12g total fat (1.9g saturated fat); 1405kJ (336 cal); 46g carbohydrate; 8.8g protein; 3.6g fibre*

If you can't find orecchiette, use penne or farfelle pasta.

salade niçoise

pasta salad

gado gado

4 medium carrots (480g), cut into batons
1 medium potato (200g), chopped coarsely
200g cauliflower, cut into florets
100g snow peas, trimmed, halved
1 lebanese cucumber (130g), cut into batons
1½ cups (100g) coarsely chopped iceberg lettuce
1½ cups (120g) bean sprouts
½ cup coarsely chopped fresh coriander

peanut sauce
½ cup (70g) roasted unsalted peanuts
2 cloves garlic, quartered
4 green onions, chopped coarsely
½ teaspoon brown sugar
1 tablespoon soy sauce
½ teaspoon chilli powder
1 tablespoon lemon juice
¾ cup (180ml) water
140ml can light coconut milk

1 Boil, steam or microwave carrot, potato, cauliflower and peas, separately, until just tender; drain. Rinse under cold water; drain.

2 Meanwhile, make peanut sauce.

3 Place carrot, potato, cauliflower and peas in large bowl with cucumber, lettuce, sprouts and coriander; toss gently to combine. Serve salad drizzled with peanut sauce.

peanut sauce Using mortar and pestle, grind nuts until crushed finely; transfer to small bowl. Using mortar and pestle, crush garlic and green onion into a coarse paste. Cook garlic mixture in medium lightly oiled frying pan, stirring, 2 minutes. Add remaining ingredients; bring to the boil. Reduce heat; simmer, uncovered, 3 minutes. Add nuts; simmer, uncovered, 5 minutes.

pre & cook time *45 minutes* serves *4*
nutritional count per serving *9.8g total fat (8.8g saturated fat); 1208kJ (289 cal); 20.3g carbohydrate; 11.1g protein; 9.2g fibre*

chicken larb

chicken salad

chicken larb

2 tablespoons long-grain white rice
1 tablespoon peanut oil
1 tablespoon finely chopped fresh lemon grass
2 fresh small red thai chillies, chopped finely
2 cloves garlic, crushed
3cm piece fresh galangal (15g), chopped finely
750g chicken mince
1 lebanese cucumber (130g), seeded, sliced thinly
1 small red onion (100g), sliced thinly
100g bean sprouts
½ cup loosely packed fresh thai basil leaves
1 cup loosely packed fresh coriander leaves
4 large iceberg lettuce leaves

dressing
⅓ cup (80ml) lime juice
2 tablespoons fish sauce
2 tablespoons kecap manis
2 tablespoons peanut oil
2 teaspoons grated palm sugar
½ teaspoon sambal oelek

1   Heat dry wok; stir-fry rice until lightly browned.
Blend or process (or crush using mortar and pestle)
rice until it resembles fine breadcrumbs.

2   Heat oil in same wok; stir-fry lemon grass, chilli,
garlic and galangal until fragrant. Remove from wok.
Stir-fry chicken, in batches, until changed in colour
and cooked through.

3   Place ingredients for dressing in screw-top jar;
shake well.

4   Return chicken and lemon grass mixture to wok
with about one-third of the dressing; stir-fry about
5 minutes or until mixture thickens slightly.

5   Place remaining dressing in large bowl with chicken,
cucumber, onion, sprouts and herbs; toss gently to
combine. Place lettuce leaves on serving plates; divide
larb salad among leaves, sprinkle with ground rice.

prep & cook time *45 minutes*   serves *4*
nutritional count per serving   *29.1g total fat (7g
saturated fat); 1986kJ (475 cal); 12.1g carbohydrate;
40.2g protein; 2.9g fibre*

chicken salad

1 litre (4 cups) boiling water
1 litre (4 cups) chicken stock
700g chicken breast fillets
1 long french bread stick (300g), sliced thinly
2 tablespoons olive oil
½ cup (150g) mayonnaise
½ cup (120g) sour cream
2 tablespoons lemon juice
4 stalks celery (600g), trimmed, sliced thinly
1 medium white onion (150g), chopped finely
3 large dill pickles (150g), sliced thinly
2 tablespoons finely chopped fresh flat-leaf parsley
1 tablespoon finely chopped fresh tarragon
1 large butter lettuce, leaves separated

1   Bring the water and stock to the boil in large frying pan;
poach chicken, covered, about 10 minutes or until cooked
through. Cool chicken in liquid 10 minutes; slice thinly.
Discard liquid.

2   Meanwhile, brush both sides of bread slices with oil;
toast under preheated grill until browned lightly both sides.

3   Whisk mayonnaise, cream and juice in small bowl.

4   Place chicken in large bowl with celery, onion, pickle and
herbs; toss gently to combine.

5   Place lettuce leaves on serving platter; top with salad and
bread, drizzle with mayonnaise mixture.

prep & cook time *50 minutes*   serves *4*
nutritional count per serving   *41.1g total fat (12.5g saturated
fat); 3352kJ (802 cal); 53.3g carbohydrate; 51.9g protein;
6.5g fibre*

vegetable salads

39

roasted mixed tomato salad, page 42

Some of the loveliest salads in the world
are vegetable salads – and many of them
can be served as an elegant first course –
iceberg lettuce with blue cheese dressing,
for example, is simple but stunning.

roasted mixed tomato salad

4 small red tomatoes (360g), halved
4 small green tomatoes (360g), halved
250g cherry tomatoes
200g red teardrop tomatoes
200g yellow teardrop tomatoes
2 tablespoons olive oil
2 tablespoons balsamic vinegar
2 tablespoons small fresh basil leaves
1 tablespoon fresh oregano leaves
1 tablespoon fresh thyme leaves

1 Preheat oven to 240°C/220°C fan-forced.

2 Combine tomatoes and oil in large shallow baking dish. Roast, uncovered, 10 minutes. Remove from oven; cool 30 minutes.

3 Place tomato mixture and remaining ingredients in large bowl; toss gently to combine.

prep & cook time *20 minutes (+ cooling)* **serves** *8*
nutritional count per serving *3g total fat (0.4g saturated fat); 167kJ (40 cal); 1.9g carbohydrate; 0.8g protein; 1.3g fibre*

pumpkin & white bean salad

1¼ cups (250g) dried white beans
1kg pumpkin, cut into 3cm pieces
250g rocket, trimmed
1 cup loosely packed fresh coriander leaves
1 tablespoon sunflower seeds

preserved lemon dressing
¼ cup (60ml) lemon juice
2 teaspoons finely chopped fresh chives
2 teaspoons finely chopped preserved lemon rind
1 teaspoon olive oil
½ teaspoon white sugar

1 Place beans in medium bowl, cover with water; stand overnight, drain. Rinse under cold water; drain. Place beans in medium saucepan of boiling water; return to the boil. Reduce heat; simmer, covered, about 15 minutes or until beans are tender. Drain. Rinse under cold water; drain.

2 Preheat oven to 220°C/200°C fan-forced.

3 Place pumpkin, in single layer, on oven tray lined with baking paper; roast about 40 minutes or until tender.

4 Meanwhile, place ingredients for preserved lemon dressing in screw-top jar; shake well.

5 Combine beans, pumpkin and dressing in large bowl with rocket and coriander. Serve salad sprinkled with seeds.

prep & cook time *1 hour 10 minutes (+ standing)* **serves** *4*
nutritional count per serving *4.4g total fat (0.9g saturated fat); 1091kJ (261 cal); 31.8g carbohydrate; 17.1g protein; 12.4g fibre*

pumpkin & white bean salad

lemon, garlic & chilli potato salad

1kg baby new potatoes, unpeeled,
   cut into 1cm slices
½ cup coarsely chopped fresh flat-leaf parsley
¼ cup coarsely chopped fresh chives

lemon and chilli butter
100g butter, softened
2 cloves garlic, crushed
1 tablespoon finely grated lemon rind
1 teaspoon dried chilli flakes

1 Combine ingredients for lemon and chilli butter in
small bowl.

2 Boil, steam or microwave potato until tender; drain.

3 Combine hot potato, lemon and chilli butter, parsley
and chives in large bowl.

prep & cook time *30 minutes* serves *6*
nutritional count per serving *13.9g total fat (9g
saturated fat); 995kJ (238 cal); 22.2g carbohydrate;
4.3g protein; 3.9g fibre*

basil pesto potato salad

1kg baby new potatoes, unpeeled, quartered
½ cup (150g) mayonnaise
2 green onions, sliced thinly
¼ cup finely sliced fresh basil
2 teaspoons finely grated lemon rind

basil pesto
½ cup firmly packed fresh basil leaves
¼ cup (20g) coarsely grated parmesan cheese
2 tablespoons roasted pine nuts
1 clove garlic, quartered
⅓ cup (80ml) olive oil

1 Boil, steam or microwave potato until tender; drain.

2 Meanwhile, make basil pesto.

3 Combine mayonnaise and pesto in large bowl; add onions
and hot potato, mix gently.

4 Serve salad topped with combined basil and rind.

basil pesto Process basil, cheese, nuts and garlic until
chopped finely. With motor operating, gradually add oil in
a thin, steady stream; process until almost smooth.

prep & cook time *30 minutes* serves *6*
nutritional count per serving *24.8g total fat (3.6g saturated
fat); 1513kJ (362 cal); 27.1g carbohydrate; 6.3g protein;
4.1g fibre*

lemon, garlic & chilli potato salad

basil pesto potato salad

german potato salad

horseradish & potato salad

german potato salad

1kg potatoes, unpeeled, cut into 2cm cubes
4 rindless bacon rashers (260g), sliced thinly
1 medium red onion (170g), sliced thinly
1 teaspoon black mustard seeds
⅔ cup finely chopped fresh flat-leaf parsley

sweet dijon dressing
¼ cup (60ml) cider vinegar
¼ cup (60ml) olive oil
1 tablespoon dijon mustard
½ teaspoon caster sugar

1 Boil, steam or microwave potato until tender; drain.

2 Meanwhile, place ingredients for sweet dijon dressing in screw-top jar; shake well.

3 Cook bacon in heated medium frying pan until crisp; drain on absorbent paper. Cook onion in same pan, stirring, until softened. Add mustard seeds; cook, stirring, 1 minute.

4 Combine potato, bacon, onion mixture, parsley and dressing in large bowl.

prep & cook time *30 minutes* serves *6*
nutritional count per serving *15.1g total fat (3.4g saturated fat); 1221kJ (292 cal); 24g carbohydrate; 13g protein; 4.1g fibre*

horseradish & potato salad

1kg large kipfler potatoes
1¼ cups (300g) sour cream
¼ cup (60ml) lemon juice
2 tablespoons prepared horseradish
2 tablespoons coarsely chopped fresh tarragon
2 stalks celery (300g), trimmed, sliced thinly
40g baby rocket leaves

1 Scrub and peel potatoes; cut lengthways into 5mm slices. Boil, steam or microwave potato until tender; drain.

2 Meanwhile, combine sour cream, juice, horseradish and tarragon in large bowl. Add celery and hot potato; toss gently to combine.

3 Serve salad topped with rocket.

prep & cook time *20 minutes* serves *6*
nutritional count per serving *20.9g total fat (13.5g saturated fat); 1329kJ (318 cal); 25.1g carbohydrate; 5.8g protein; 4.2g fibre*

raw pumpkin, pomegranate & pepita salad

500g piece butternut pumpkin
½ cup (125ml) pomegranate pulp
80g baby spinach leaves
1 tablespoon pepitas

red wine vinegar dressing
2 tablespoons red wine vinegar
1 teaspoon olive oil
1 teaspoon dijon mustard

1 Using mandolin or V-slicer, cut pumpkin into paper-thin slices.

2 Place ingredients for red wine vinegar dressing in screw-top jar; shake well.

3 Place pumpkin and dressing in large bowl with pomegranate and spinach; toss gently to combine. Serve salad sprinkled with pepitas.

prep time *15 minutes* serves 4
nutritional count per serving *3.2g total fat (0.6g saturated fat); 422kJ (101 cal); 11.9g carbohydrate; 4g protein; 4.2g fibre*

warm squash & zucchini salad with leek dressing

8 medium yellow patty-pan squash (240g), quartered
12 baby zucchini (200g)

leek dressing
2 teaspoons olive oil
1 small leek (200g), sliced thinly
2 tablespoons lemon juice
1 tablespoon vegetable stock
1 tablespoon rice vinegar
2 teaspoons lemon thyme leaves

1 Make leek dressing.

2 Meanwhile, cook squash and zucchini in medium baking-paper-lined steamer, over medium saucepan of simmering water, about 5 minutes or until tender.

3 Serve vegetables drizzled with leek dressing.

leek dressing Heat oil in small frying pan; cook leek, stirring, about 10 minutes or until tender. Remove from heat; stir in remaining ingredients.

prep & cook time *15 minutes* serves *4*
nutritional count per serving *2.7g total fat (0.3g saturated fat); 247kJ (59 cal); 4.3g carbohydrate; 2.9g protein; 3.1g fibre*

kumara & orange salad

2 medium kumara (800g), cut into wedges
2 tablespoons olive oil
1 teaspoon ground cumin
½ teaspoon ground nutmeg
½ cup (100g) couscous
½ cup (125ml) boiling water
2 medium oranges (480g), segmented
½ cup (65g) dried cranberries
⅓ cup (40g) pecans, roasted

orange balsamic dressing
1 tablespoon orange juice
1 tablespoon balsamic vinegar
1 teaspoon dijon mustard
1 clove garlic, crushed
2 tablespoons olive oil

1 Preheat oven to 220°C/200°C fan-forced.

2 Combine kumara, oil, cumin and nutmeg on oven tray; roast, uncovered, about 25 minutes or until kumara is tender.

3 Meanwhile, combine couscous with the water in large heatproof bowl; cover, stand about 5 minutes or until water is absorbed.

4 Place ingredients for orange balsamic dressing in screw-top jar; shake well.

5 Combine orange, cranberries and pecans with couscous. Serve kumara with couscous and dressing.

prep & cook time *45 minutes* serves *4*
nutritional count per serving *21.3g total fat (2.4g saturated fat); 1856kJ (444 cal); 51.5g carbohydrate; 8.4g protein; 6.3g fibre*

leaf salad with cranberry dressing

1 baby cos lettuce (180g), trimmed, leaves separated
250g rocket, trimmed
1 small radicchio (150g), trimmed, leaves separated
½ cup (40g) flaked almonds, roasted
½ cup (65g) dried cranberries

cranberry dressing
¼ cup (60m) olive oil
¼ cup (60ml) red wine vinegar
2 tablespoons cranberry juice
2 teaspoons dijon mustard
1 clove garlic, crushed
2 tablespoons cranberry sauce
½ small red onion (50g), chopped finely

1 Make cranberry dressing.

2 Combine lettuce, rocket and radicchio in large serving bowl; sprinkle with nuts and cranberries, drizzle with dressing.

cranberry dressing Blend oil, vinegar, juice, mustard, garlic and sauce until combined; stir in onion.

prep time *15 minutes* serves *6*
nutritional count per serving *13.4g total fat (1.5g saturated fat); 828kJ (198 cal); 14.3g carbohydrate; 3.7g protein; 3.1g fibre*

kumara & orange salad

leaf salad with cranberry dressing

warm potato & beetroot salad

5 medium potatoes (1kg), halved
¼ cup (60ml) olive oil
2 tablespoons balsamic vinegar
½ small red onion (50g), chopped finely
¼ cup (50g) drained baby capers, rinsed
850g can baby beetroot, drained, quartered
3 hard-boiled eggs, quartered

1 Preheat oven to 220°C/200°C fan-forced.

2 Cook potato in large saucepan of boiling water 5 minutes; drain. Cut potato into wedges, combine with 1 tablespoon of the oil on oven tray. Roast, uncovered, about 45 minutes or until potato is browned lightly.

3 Meanwhile, whisk vinegar and remaining oil in small bowl.

4 Place potato in large bowl with onion, capers and beetroot; drizzle with dressing. Top salad with egg; serve warm.

prep & cook time *1 hour* serves *4*
nutritional count per serving *18g total fat (3.1g saturated fat); 1777kJ (425 cal); 48g carbohydrate; 13.2g protein; 9.1g fibre*

cabbage, orange & radish salad

1 medium orange (240g)
2 cups (160g) finely shredded green cabbage
2 red radishes (70g), trimmed, sliced thinly
½ cup loosely packed fresh mint leaves

cumin and orange dressing
1 teaspoon cumin seeds
¼ teaspoon hot paprika
2 tablespoons olive oil
1 tablespoon white balsamic vinegar

1 Segment orange over small bowl; reserve 1 tablespoon juice for dressing.

2 Make cumin and orange dressing.

3 Place orange segments and dressing in large bowl with remaining ingredients; toss gently to combine.

cumin and orange dressing Dry-fry spices in heated small frying pan until fragrant; cool. Place spices in screw-top jar with oil, vinegar and reserved orange juice; shake well.

prep & cook time *25 minutes* serves *4*
nutritional count per serving *9.3g total fat (1.3g saturated fat); 472kJ (113 cal); 5g carbohydrate; 1.3g protein; 2.9g fibre*

warm red cabbage & bacon salad

2 rindless bacon rashers (130g), chopped coarsely
1 tablespoon olive oil
6 cups (480g) coarsely shredded red cabbage
2 tablespoons red wine vinegar
1 tablespoon brown sugar
½ cup coarsely chopped fresh flat-leaf parsley

1 Cook bacon in heated large frying pan until crisp. Drain on absorbent paper.

2 Heat oil in same pan; cook cabbage, stirring, about 5 minutes or until softened. Add vinegar and sugar; cook, stirring, about 10 minutes or until liquid evaporates.

3 Return bacon to pan; cook, stirring, until heated through. Remove from heat; stir in parsley.

prep & cook time *25 minutes* serves *4*
nutritional count per serving *9.2g total fat (2.2g saturated fat); 656kJ (157 cal); 7g carbohydrate; 9.1g protein; 5g fibre*

cabbage, orange & radish salad

warm red cabbage & bacon salad

cos, avocado & tomato salad

tomato, onion & cucumber salad

cos, avocado & tomato salad

1 baby cos lettuce
3 medium tomatoes (450g), chopped finely
2 medium avocados (500g), chopped finely
1 lebanese cucumber (130g), chopped finely
1 small red onion (100g), chopped finely
¼ cup coarsely chopped fresh coriander
¼ cup (60ml) lime juice
2 cloves garlic, crushed

1 Separate lettuce leaves. Reserve several of the larger leaves; shred remaining leaves coarsely.

2 Place shredded lettuce in medium bowl with remaining ingredients; toss gently to combine. Serve salad divided among reserved leaves.

prep time *15 minutes* serves *4*
nutritional count per serving *20.2g total fat (4.3g saturated fat); 970kJ (232 cal); 5.8g carbohydrate; 4.3g protein; 4.8g fibre*

tomato, onion & cucumber salad

4 large egg tomatoes (360g), sliced thinly into rounds
1 small red onion (100g), sliced thinly
2 lebanese cucumbers (260g), peeled, sliced thinly into rounds
2 tablespoons white wine vinegar
1 tablespoon olive oil
1 teaspoon white sugar
¼ cup small fresh basil leaves

1 Layer tomato, onion and cucumber in large serving bowl.

2 Drizzle with combined vinegar, oil and sugar. Serve sprinkled with basil leaves.

prep time *10 minutes* serves *4*
nutritional count per serving *4.7g total fat (0.6g saturated fat); 322kJ (77 cal); 5.9g carbohydrate; 1.6g protein; 2.4g fibre*

green bean & tomato salad

200g green beans, trimmed
250g cherry tomatoes, halved

mustard hazelnut dressing
½ cup (70g) roasted hazelnuts, skinned,
   chopped coarsely
2 tablespoons hazelnut oil
2 tablespoons cider vinegar
1 teaspoon wholegrain mustard

1 Place ingredients for mustard hazelnut dressing in
screw-top jar; shake well.

2 Boil, steam or microwave beans until tender; drain.
Rinse under cold water; drain.

3 Place beans and dressing in medium bowl with
tomatoes; toss gently to combine.

prep & cook time *20 minutes* serves *4*
nutritional count per serving *20.2g total fat (1.8g
saturated fat); 920kJ (220 cal); 3.6g carbohydrate;
4.2g protein; 4.3g fibre*

broad bean, corn & capsicum salad

1 medium red capsicum (200g)
1 fresh long red chilli
300g frozen broad beans
2 trimmed corn cobs (500g)
1 cup loosely packed fresh flat-leaf parsley leaves

garlic dressing
1 clove garlic, crushed
1 teaspoon caster sugar
¼ cup (60ml) white wine vinegar
1 tablespoon olive oil

1 Quarter capsicum; discard seeds and membranes. Halve
chilli lengthways. Cook capsicum and chilli on heated, oiled
grill plate (or grill or barbecue), skin-side down, until skin
blackens. Chop chilli finely. Cover capsicum for 5 minutes;
peel away skin, chop coarsely.

2 Boil, steam or microwave beans until tender; drain.
Rinse under cold water; drain. Peel away grey outer shells.

3 Place ingredients for garlic dressing in screw-top jar;
shake well.

4 Cook corn on grill plate until tender; cut into thick slices.

5 Place capsicum, beans and corn in large bowl with
dressing, chilli and parsley; toss gently to combine.

prep & cook time *30 minutes* serves *4*
nutritional count per serving *6g total fat (0.7g saturated fat);
886kJ (2121 cal); 24.1g carbohydrate; 8.9g protein; 11.7g fibre*

green bean & tomato salad

broad bean, corn & capsicum salad

Chopped salad ingredients vary from recipe to recipe, the only common rule is that all the ingredients are 'chopped'. You can also place all of the roughly chopped ingredients on a large chopping board and use a large knife to chop them all together.

chopped salad

1 cos lettuce, shredded coarsely
1 raddicchio, shredded coarsely
1 large red capsicum (350g), chopped coarsely
1 small red onion (100g), chopped finely
1 lebanese cucumber (130g), chopped coarsely
3 large egg tomatoes (270g), chopped coarsely
2 celery stalks (300g), trimmed, chopped finely
2 red radishes (70g), trimmed, sliced thinly
1 cup coarsely chopped fresh flat-leaf parsley
½ cup coarsely chopped fresh basil
150g fetta cheese, crumbled
2 tablespoons red wine vinegar
2 tablespoons extra virgin olive oil

1 Place ingredients in large serving bowl; toss gently to combine.

prep time *15 minutes*   serves *4*
nutritional count per serving *19g total fat (7g saturated fat); 1208kJ (289 cal); 11.9g carbohydrate; 13.4g protein; 9.9g fibre*

celeriac remoulade

⅓ cup (100g) mayonnaise
1 clove garlic, crushed
⅓ cup (80g) sour cream
2 tablespoons lemon juice
2 teaspoons dijon mustard
650g celeriac, trimmed, grated coarsely
½ cup coarsely chopped fresh flat-leaf parsley

1 Combine mayonnaise in medium bowl with garlic, sour cream, juice and mustard.

2 Add celeriac and parsley; mix gently.

prep time *10 minutes* serves *4*
nutritional count per serving *16.3g total fat (6.2g saturated fat); 920kJ (220 cal); 12.3g carbohydrate; 3.1g protein; 6.4g fibre*

mixed bean salad

250g green beans, trimmed
250g yellow beans, trimmed
60g butter, chopped
⅓ cup (45g) finely chopped roasted hazelnuts
½ cup coarsely chopped fresh flat-leaf parsley
2 teaspoons finely grated lemon rind

1 Boil, steam or microwave beans until tender; drain.

2 Place warm beans in medium bowl with remaining ingredients: toss gently to combine.

prep & cook time *15 minutes* serves *4*
nutritional count per serving *19.5g total fat (8.4g saturated at); 907kJ (217 cal); 3.8g carbohydrate; 4.7g protein; 5g fibre*

green, yellow & broad bean salad

150g green beans, trimmed
150g yellow beans, trimmed
300g frozen broad beans
2 tablespoons olive oil
2 tablespoons lemon juice

lemon chilli breadcrumbs
25g butter
1 tablespoon finely grated lemon rind
⅓ cup (25g) stale breadcrumbs
¼ teaspoon chilli powder

1 Make lemon chilli breadcrumbs.

2 Boil, steam or microwave green, yellow and broad beans, separately, until tender; drain. Rinse under cold water; drain. Peel away grey outer shells from broad beans.

3 Combine all beans in medium bowl with oil and juice; sprinkle with breadcrumbs.

lemon chilli breadcrumbs Melt butter in small frying pan; cook remaining ingredients over low heat, stirring, until crumbs brown.

prep & cook time *25 minutes* serves *6*
nutritional count per serving *10g total fat (3.2g saturated fat); 594kJ (142 cal);5.3g carbohydrate; 5.2g protein; 4.8g fibre*

rocket & parmesan salad

1 tablespoon balsamic vinegar
1 tablespoon olive oil
100g baby rocket leaves
2 tablespoons roasted pine nuts
40g drained semi-dried tomatoes, chopped coarsely
⅓ cup (25g) flaked parmesan

1 Place ingredients in large bowl; toss gently to combine.

prep time *10 minutes* serves *4*
nutritional count per serving *12.3g total fat (2.3g saturated fat); 635kJ (152 cal); 4.4g carbohydrate; 5.1g protein; 2.2g fibre*

celeriac remoulade

green, yellow & broad bean salad

mixed bean salad

rocket & parmesan salad

cauliflower & green olive salad

1 small cauliflower (1kg), trimmed, cut into florets
1 cup (120g) large green olives, seeded, halved
1 stalk celery (150g), trimmed, sliced thinly
1 cup loosely packed celery leaves
½ cup loosely packed fresh flat-leaf parsley leaves
1 small red onion (100g), sliced thinly
2 tablespoons lemon juice
1 tablespoon finely chopped preserved lemon
2 tablespoons olive oil
1 clove garlic, crushed
125g fetta cheese, crumbled

1 Boil, steam or microwave cauliflower until tender; drain.

2 Place cauliflower in medium bowl with olives, celery, celery leaves, parsley, onion, juice, preserved lemon, oil and garlic; toss gently until combined.

3 Serve salad sprinkled with cheese.

prep & cook time *25 minutes* serves 4
nutritional count per serving *17.2g total fat (6.1g saturated fat); 1087kJ (260 cal); 12.3g carbohydrate; 11.3g protein; 5.5g fibre*

rainbow salad

600g baby beetroot, trimmed
300g asparagus, trimmed
2 cloves garlic, crushed
1 tablespoon finely grated lemon rind
2 small avocados (400g), cut into thin wedges
3 medium oranges (720g), segmented
1 medium red onion (170g), sliced thinly

wholegrain mustard dressing
1 tablespoon wholegrain mustard
1 tablespoon cider vinegar
1 tablespoon finely chopped fresh chives
¼ cup coarsely chopped fresh flat-leaf parsley

1   Preheat oven to 180°C/160°C fan-forced.

2   Place beetroot on oven tray; roast uncovered, about 45 minutes or until beetroot is tender. Cool 10 minutes. Peel beetroot; cut in quarters.

3   Meanwhile, combine asparagus, garlic and rind on oven tray; roast, uncovered, about 10 minutes or until asparagus is tender. Cut asparagus in half, crossways.

4   Combine ingredients for wholegrain mustard dressing in small bowl.

5   Place beetroot and asparagus mixture in large bowl with remaining ingredients and dressing; toss gently to combine.

prep & cook time *1 hour*   serves 4
nutritional count per serving *16.3g total fat (3.4g saturated fat); 1166kJ (279 cal); 25.3g carbohydrate; 8g protein; 10.1g fibre*

eggplant, tomato & parsley salad

cooking-oil spray
2 large eggplants (1kg), cut into 1cm slices
2 large tomatoes (440g), chopped finely
1 cup coarsely chopped fresh flat-leaf parsley

mint yogurt dressing
½ cup (140g) low-fat natural yogurt
2 tablespoons water
1 tablespoon mint sauce
1 tablespoon finely chopped fresh mint

1 Spray heated barbecue grill plate with cooking-oil spray for 2 seconds. Cook eggplant, about 2 minutes each side, until tender.

2 Meanwhile, combine ingredients for mint yogurt dressing in small bowl.

3 Divide eggplant, tomato and parsley among serving plates; drizzle with dressing.

prep & cook time *20 minutes*   serves *4*
nutritional count per serving *1.5g total fat (0.1g saturated fat); 426kJ (102 cal); 11.8g carbohydrate; 6.3g protein; 7.9g fibre*

winter vegetable coleslaw

2 cups (160g) finely shredded cabbage
1 baby fennel bulb (130g), trimmed, sliced thinly
100g green beans, trimmed, sliced thinly
600g celeriac, peeled, grated coarsely
1 stalk celery (150g), trimmed, sliced thinly
1 cup loosely packed fresh flat-leaf parsley leaves

cider dressing
¼ cup (60ml) olive oil
2 tablespoons cider vinegar
1 teaspoon caster sugar
1 teaspoon dijon mustard

1 Place ingredients for cider dressing in screw-top jar; shake well.

2 Place cabbage and fennel in large bowl with remaining salad ingredients and dressing; toss gently to combine.

prep time *25 minutes* serves *4*
nutritional count per serving *14.2g total fat (1.9g saturated fat); 941kJ (225 cal); 15.2g carbohydrate; 3.5g protein; 12.3g fibre*

potato salad with artichoke hearts

1kg kipfler potatoes, halved lengthways
1 tablespoon olive oil
8 cloves garlic, halved
340g jar artichoke hearts, drained, quartered
1 cup firmly packed fresh flat-leaf parsley leaves

creamy mustard dressing
1 tablespoon balsamic vinegar
1 tablespoon american mustard
½ cup (125ml) cream

1 Place ingredients for creamy mustard dressing in screw-top jar; shake well.

2 Boil, steam or microwave potato until tender; drain. Combine potato and oil in medium bowl.

3 Cook potato, garlic and artichoke, in batches, on heated oiled grill plate (or grill or barbecue) until potato is browned.

4 Return vegetables to same bowl with parsley; toss gently to combine. Serve salad drizzled with dressing.

prep & cook time *25 minutes* serves *4*
nutritional count per serving *18.8g total fat (9.6g saturated fat); 1522kJ (364 cal); 35.4g carbohydrate; 8.6g protein; 8.5g fibre*

winter vegetable coleslaw

potato salad with artichoke hearts

iceberg lettuce with blue cheese dressing

1 small iceberg lettuce, trimmed, cut into 6 wedges
150g blue cheese, chopped
¼ cup (75g) mayonnaise
¼ cup (60ml) buttermilk
2 tablespoons lemon juice
2 tablespoons water
¼ cup finely chopped chives

1 Place lettuce wedges on serving plate.

2 Blend or process cheese, mayonnaise, buttermilk, juice and the water until smooth. Stir in chives. Drizzle dressing over lettuce.

prep time *10 minutes* serves *6*
nutritional count per serving *12.4g total fat (5.8g saturated fat); 635kJ (152 cal); 3.5g carbohydrate; 6.2g protein; 1g fibre*

roasted beetroot & potato salad

pepita & oak leaf lettuce salad

roasted beetroot & potato salad

1 tablespoon olive oil
3 medium beetroots (500g), peeled,
    cut into 3cm pieces
400g baby new potatoes
2 rindless bacon rashers (130g), chopped coarsely
100g baby rocket leaves, trimmed

paprika mayonnaise
½ cup (150g) mayonnaise
1 tablespoon lemon juice
4 sweet gherkins (35g), chopped coarsely
1 teaspoon sweet paprika
1 clove garlic, crushed

1 Preheat oven to 200°C/180°C fan-forced.

2 Combine oil, beetroot and potatoes in large shallow
baking dish. Roast, turning occasionally, about 30 minutes
or until vegetables are almost tender.

3 Add bacon to dish; cook about 10 minutes or until
bacon is crisp. Remove dish from oven; stand 10 minutes.
Halve unpeeled potatoes; drain bacon.

4 Whisk ingredients for paprika mayonnaise in small bowl.

5 Place vegetables and bacon in large bowl with rocket;
toss gently. Serve salad with mayonnaise.

prep & cook time *45 minutes* serves *6*
nutritional count per serving *13g total fat (2g saturated
fat); 974kJ (233 cal); 21.2g carbohydrate; 6g protein;
3.9g fibre*

pepita & oak leaf lettuce salad

⅓ cup (65g) roasted pepitas
1 green oak leaf lettuce, leaves separated
1 small red onion (100g), sliced thinly

cranberry dressing
2 tablespoons olive oil
2 tablespoons red wine vinegar
2 tablespoons cranberry sauce

1 Place ingredients for cranberry dressing in screw-top jar;
shake well.

2 Place salad ingredients in medium bowl with dressing;
toss gently to combine.

prep time *10 minutes* serves *4*
nutritional count per serving *9.8g total fat (0.9g saturated
fat); 464kJ (111 cal); 4.4g carbohydrate; 0.7g protein; 2g fibre*

pulse, pasta & grain
salads

red lentil patty salad, page 78

These are the heavy lifters of the salad family, there are no delicate flowers here. They're hearty and filling and packed with protein and carbohydrates. All of them make fine main course dishes.

red lentil patty salad

1 cup (200g) red lentils
¼ cup (40g) burghul
½ cup (125ml) boiling water
1 small brown onion (80g), chopped coarsely
2 cloves garlic, quartered
⅔ cup (100g) plain flour
1 egg
1 cup (100g) packaged breadcrumbs
2 tablespoons olive oil
1 cup loosely packed fresh flat-leaf parsley leaves
3 medium tomatoes (450g) cut into wedges
1 lebanese cucumber (130g), chopped coarsely
1 medium avocado (250g), chopped coarsely
1 small green capsicum (150g), sliced thinly

lemon yogurt dressing
1 cup (280g) yogurt
2 teaspoons finely grated lemon rind
2 tablespoons lemon juice

1 Cook lentils in medium saucepan of boiling water until tender; drain, cool.

2 Meanwhile, place burghul in small heatproof bowl; cover with the boiling water. Stand 10 minutes.

3 Blend or process lentils, onion and garlic until smooth; transfer to medium bowl. Stir in burghul, flour, egg and breadcrumbs. Refrigerate 1 hour or until firm.

4 Meanwhile, combine ingredients for lemon yogurt dressing in small bowl.

5 Shape lentil mixture into 20 patties. Heat oil in large frying pan; cook patties until browned. Drain on absorbent paper.

6 Place patties in large bowl with remaining ingredients; toss gently to combine. Drizzle with dressing.

prep & cook time *20 minutes (+ standing & refrigeration)* serves *4*
nutritional count per serving *25.3g total fat (5.8g saturated fat); 2675kJ (640 cal); 68g carbohydrate; 27.6g protein; 14.4g fibre*

chickpea, pumpkin & fetta salad

800g butternut pumpkin, cut into 1cm pieces
1 tablespoon olive oil
2 cloves garlic, sliced thinly
2 x 400g cans chickpeas, rinsed, drained
200g fetta cheese, crumbled
1 cup firmly packed fresh coriander leaves
⅓ cup (65g) pepitas

roasted chilli dressing
4 fresh long red chillies, halved lengthways
2 tablespoons rice vinegar
2 tablespoons lime juice
1 tablespoon olive oil

1 Preheat oven to 200°C/180°C fan-forced.

2 Combine pumpkin, oil and garlic in large shallow baking dish. Roast, uncovered, turning occasionally, about 30 minutes or until pumpkin is tender.

3 Meanwhile, make roasted chilli dressing.

4 Place pumpkin in large bowl with remaining ingredients and dressing; toss gently to cobine.

roasted chilli dressing Cook chilli, skin-side up, under hot grill until skin blackens. Cover chilli pieces for 5 minutes; peel then chop finely. Place chilli and remaining ingredients in screw-top jar; shake well.

prep & cook time *40 minutes*   serves *4*
nutritional count per serving *31.7g total fat (11.2g saturated fat); 2195kJ (525 cal); 32.3g carbohydrate; 25.2g protein; 9.5g fibre*

chickpea, pumpkin & fetta salad

fennel & tomato couscous salad

250g cherry tomatoes, halved
cooking-oil spray
1 cup (200g) couscous
1 cup (250ml) boiling water
2 baby fennel bulbs (260g), trimmed, sliced thinly
¼ cup (60ml) olive oil
1 tablespoon white wine vinegar
1 clove garlic, crushed
2 tablespoons finely chopped fresh oregano

1 Preheat oven to 200°C/180°C fan-forced. Place tomato on oven tray; spray with oil. Roast 10 minutes or until skins burst.

2 Meanwhile, combine couscous with the water in medium heatproof bowl, cover; stand about 5 minutes or until water is absorbed, fluffing with fork occasionally.

3 Stir tomato and remaining ingredients into couscous.

prep & cook time *20 minutes* serves *4*
nutritional count per serving *14.8g total fat (2g saturated fat); 1384kJ (331 cal); 40.8g carbohydrate; 7.1g protein; 2.7g fibre*

curried couscous & chickpea salad

½ cup (125ml) water
½ cup (125ml) chicken stock
1 teaspoon curry powder
1 cup (200g) couscous
400g can chickpeas, rinsed, drained
200g fetta cheese, crumbled
½ cup coarsely chopped fresh coriander
2 green onions, sliced thinly
1 teaspoon finely grated lemon rind
¼ cup (60ml) lemon juice

1 Bring the water, stock and curry powder to the boil in small saucepan.

2 Combine couscous in medium heatproof bowl with stock mixture, cover; stand about 5 minutes or until water is absorbed, fluffing with fork occasionally.

3 Stir remaining ingredients into couscous.

prep & cook time *15 minutes* serves *4*
nutritional count per serving *13.6g total fat (8g saturated fat); 1701kJ (407 cal); 48.7g carbohydrate; 20.2g protein; 4g fibre*

orange & date couscous salad

1 cup (200g) couscous
1 cup (250ml) boiling water
2 medium oranges (480g)
40g baby spinach leaves
½ small red onion (50g), sliced thinly
½ cup seeded fresh dates (70g), sliced thinly
1 tablespoon olive oil

1 Combine couscous with the water in medium heatproof bowl, cover; stand about 5 minutes or until water is absorbed, fluffing with fork occasionally.

2 Meanwhile, coarsely grate rind from both oranges. Segment oranges over small bowl; reserve any juice in bowl (you need ¼ cup juice). Stir orange segments, reserved juice and remaining ingredients into couscous.

prep time *15 minutes* serves *4*
nutritional count per serving *5.1g total fat (0.7g saturated fat); 1329kJ (318 cal); 56.7g carbohydrate; 8.2g protein; 4.9g fibre*

preserved lemon & couscous salad

1 cup (200g) couscous
1 cup (250ml) boiling water
1 teaspoon ground cumin
½ cup (75g) raisins
2 tablespoons finely chopped preserved lemon rind
1 cup coarsely chopped fresh mint
¼ cup (60ml) lemon juice

1 Combine couscous with the water in medium heatproof bowl, cover; stand about 5 minutes or until water is absorbed, fluffing with fork occasionally.

2 Stir remaining ingredients into couscous.

prep time *15 minutes* serves *4*
nutritional count per serving *0.7g total fat (0.1g saturated fat); 1066kJ (255 cal); 52.8g carbohydrate; 7.4g protein; 2.5g fibre*

fennel & tomato couscous salad

curried couscous & chickpea salad

orange & date couscous salad

preserved lemon & couscous salad

four-bean salad with mustard dressing

¼ cup (45g) dried lima beans
¼ cup (50g) dried borlotti beans
¼ cup (50g) dried kidney beans
¼ cup (50g) dried cannellini beans
125g cherry tomatoes, halved
½ small red onion (50g), sliced thinly
½ small green capsicum (75g), sliced thinly
½ cup loosely packed fresh flat-leaf parsley leaves

wholegrain mustard dressing
⅓ cup (80ml) olive oil
2 tablespoons red wine vinegar
2 teaspoons wholegrain mustard

1 Cover lima beans with cold water in medium bowl. Cover remaining beans with cold water in another medium bowl. Stand overnight; rinse, drain.

2 Cook beans, separately, in medium saucepans of boiling water until tender; drain.

3 Meanwhile, place ingredients for wholegrain mustard dressing in screw-top jar; shake well.

4 Place beans in medium bowl with remaining ingredients and dressing; toss gently to combine.

prep & cook time *1 hour (+ standing)* serves *6*
nutritional count per serving *12.8g total fat (1.8g saturated fat); 903kJ (216 cal); 15.2g carbohydrate; 7.5g protein; 5.9g fibre*

chilli, corn, tomato & chickpea salad

1 chipotle chilli
2 tablespoons boiling water
½ cup (130g) bottled tomato pasta sauce
1 tablespoon lime juice
1 teaspoon ground cumin
2 trimmed corn cobs (500g)
420g can chickpeas, drained, rinsed
250g cherry tomatoes, halved
1 small red onion (100g), sliced thinly
1 cup loosely packed fresh coriander leaves

1 Place chilli and the water in small bowl; stand 15 minutes. Discard stalk; blend or process chilli, soaking liquid and sauce until mixture is smooth. Transfer to small bowl; stir in juice.

2 Dry-fry cumin in small frying pan, stirring, until fragrant; stir into chilli sauce mixture.

3 Cook corn on heated oiled grill plate (or grill or barbecue) until browned lightly and tender. Cut kernels from cobs.

4 Combine chilli mixture and corn in large bowl with remaining ingredients.

prep & cook time *35 minutes (+ standing)* serves *4*
nutritional count per serving *2.9g total fat (0.3g saturated fat); 853kJ (204 cal); 30.5g carbohydrate; 9.5g protein; 9.4g fibre*

lemon & lime rice salad

2 cups (400g) basmati rice
½ cup (80g) almond kernels, chopped coarsely
¼ cup (50g) pepitas
¼ cup (35g) sunflower seed kernels
½ cup thinly sliced fresh coriander
½ cup thinly sliced fresh flat-leaf parsley

lemon and lime dressing
¼ cup (60ml) olive oil
¼ cup (60ml) lemon juice
1 teaspoon finely grated lime rind
2 tablespoons lime juice
¼ teaspoon cracked black pepper

1   Cook rice in large saucepan of boiling water, uncovered, until tender; drain. Rinse under cold water; drain.

2   Meanwhile, place ingredients for lemon and lime dressing in screw-top jar; shake well.

3   Place rice in large bowl with remaining ingredients and dressing; stir gently to combine.

prep & cook time *25 minutes* serves *6*
nutritional count per serving *23.6g total fat (2.8g saturated fat); 2011kJ (481 cal); 55.4g carbohydrate; 10.8g protein; 3.1g fibre*

olive & capsicum brown rice salad

2 cups (400g) brown rice
2 large red capsicums (700g)
1 cup (160g) fetta-stuffed green olives, sliced thinly
1 tablespoon finely chopped fresh oregano
1 fresh long red chilli, chopped finely

red wine vinaigrette
2 tablespoons lemon juice
2 tablespoons red wine vinegar
2 tablespoons olive oil
½ teaspoon white sugar
1 clove garlic, crushed

1   Cook rice in large saucepan of boiling water, uncovered, until tender; drain. Rinse under cold water; drain.

2   Meanwhile, quarter capsicums; discard seeds and membranes. Cook capsicum, skin-side up, under hot grill until skin blackens. Cover capsicum with plastic for 5 minutes; peel away skin then slice thinly.

3   Place ingredients for red wine vinaigrette in screw-top jar; shake well.

4   Place rice and capsicum in large bowl with remaining ingredients and vinaigrette; stir gently to combine.

prep & cook time *40 minutes* serves *6*
nutritional count per serving *10.1g total fat (1.5g saturated fat); 1496kJ (358 cal); 56.6g carbohydrate; 7g protein; 5.4g fibre*

lemon & lime rice salad

olive & capsicum brown rice salad

avocado & wasabi rice salad

wild rice salad with spinach & figs

pulse, pasta & grain salads

avocado & wasabi rice salad

2 cups (400g) jasmine rice
2 medium avocados (500g), halved, chopped coarsely
2 tablespoons lime juice
1 cup (50g) snow pea tendrils, chopped coarsely
1 sheet nori, shredded finely

wasabi dressing
¾ cup (225g) mayonnaise
2 tablespoons lime juice
2 tablespoons rice wine vinegar
3 teaspoons wasabi

1 Cook rice in large saucepan of boiling water, uncovered, until tender; drain. Rinse under cold water; drain.

2 Meanwhile, combine ingredients for wasabi dressing in small bowl.

3 Combine avocado and juice in large bowl. Add rice, dressing, tendrils and nori; stir gently to combine.

prep & cook time *25 minutes* serves *6*
nutritional count per serving *26g total fat (4.5g saturated fat); 2161kJ (517 cal); 62.9g carbohydrate; 6.8g protein; 2.3g fibre*

wild rice salad with spinach & figs

2 cups (400g) wild rice blend
¾ cup (90g) coarsely chopped pescans, roasted
½ cup (100g) thinly sliced dried figs
100g baby spinach leaves, chopped coarsely
2 green onions, sliced thinly

orange balsamic dressing
2 teaspoons finely grated orange rind
½ cup (125ml) orange juice
2 tablespoons olive oil
1 tablespoon white balsamic vinegar

1 Cook rice in large saucepan of boiling water, uncovered, until tender; drain. Rinse under cold water; drain.

2 Meanwhile, place ingredients for orange balsamic dressing in screw-top jar; shake well.

3 Place rice in large bowl with remaining ingredients and dressing; stir gently to combine.

prep & cook time *15 minutes* serves *6*
nutritional count per serving *17.4g total fat (1.6g saturated fat); 1810kJ (433 cal); 59.7g carbohydrate; 6.8g protein; 4.9g fibre*

vegetable & couscous salad

cooking-oil spray
1 medium kumara (400g), cut into 5mm slices
2 large zucchini (300g), cut into 5mm slices
1½ cups (300g) couscous
1½ cups (375ml) hot chicken stock
450g can whole baby beetroot, drained, quartered
40g baby spinach leaves
2 tablespoons coarsely chopped fresh flat-leaf parsley

orange dressing
1 teaspoon finely grated orange rind
¼ cup (60ml) orange juice
2 tablespoons white wine vinegar
1 teaspoon dijon mustard

1 Spray heated barbecue grill plate with cooking-oil spray for 2 seconds. Cook kumara and zucchini, in batches, until tender. Cool 10 minutes.

2 Meanwhile, combine couscous with stock in large heatproof bowl, cover; stand 5 minutes or until liquid is absorbed, fluffing with fork occasionally.

3 Place ingredients for orange dressing in screw-top jar; shake well.

4 Add kumara, zucchini and remaining ingredients to couscous; stir gently to combine. Serve salad drizzled with dressing.

prep & cook time *20 minutes* serves *4*
nutritional count per serving *1.8g total fat (0.3g saturated fat); 1714kJ (410 cal); 79.8g carbohydrate; 14.6g protein; 5.9g fibre*

honey mustard pasta salad

375g penne pasta
170g asparagus, trimmed, cut into 2cm lengths
4 green onions, sliced thinly
½ cup coarsely chopped fresh flat-leaf parsley

wholegrain mustard dressing
⅓ cup (80ml) buttermilk
2 teaspoons lemon juice
2 teaspoons wholegrain mustard
1 teaspoon honey

1 Cook pasta in large saucepan of boiling water until tender; drain. Rinse under cold water; drain.

2 Meanwhile, boil, steam or microwave asparagus until tender; drain. Rinse under cold water; drain.

3 Place ingredients for wholegrain mustard dressing in screw-top jar; shake well.

4 Place pasta and asparagus in large bowl with remaining ingredients and dressing; toss gently to combine.

prep & cook time *20 minutes*   serves *4*
nutritional count per serving *1.1g total fat (0.3g saturated fat); 1083kJ (259 cal); 49.8g carbohydrate; 9.5g protein; 4.5g fibre*

crispy polenta salad

1 litre (4 cups) water
1 cup (170g) polenta
½ cup (40g) coarsely grated parmesan cheese
½ cup (60g) coarsely grated cheddar cheese
1 tablespoon olive oil
80g baby spinach leaves
1 large red capsicum (350g), sliced thinly
1 small red onion (100g), sliced thinly

walnut dressing
¼ cup (60ml) walnut oil
2 tablespoons white wine vinegar
1 clove garlic, crushed
⅓ cup (35g) coarsely chopped roasted walnuts
¼ cup coarsely chopped fresh flat-leaf parsley

1 Oil 19cm x 29cm slice pan.

2 Bring the water to the boil in medium saucepan. Gradually stir in polenta; reduce heat. Simmer, stirring, about 10 minutes or until polenta thickens. Stir in cheeses; spread polenta into pan. Refrigerate 1 hour or until firm.

3 Meanwhile, place ingredients for walnut dressing in screw-top jar; shake well.

4 Turn polenta onto board; cut into quarters then cut into 1cm cubes. Heat oil in large frying pan; cook polenta until browned lightly.

5 Place polenta in large bowl with remaining ingredients and dressing; toss gently to combine.

prep & cook time *25 minutes (+ refrigeration)* **serves** *4*
nutritional count per serving *25g total fat (7.1g saturated fat); 1831kJ (438 cal); 35g carbohydrate; 16.4g protein; 4.6g fibre*

bean salad with creamy dressing

400g can butter beans, rinsed, drained
400g can borlotti beans, rinsed, drained
250g cherry tomatoes, quartered
12 cherry bocconcini cheese (180g), halved
60g baby rocket leaves
½ cup (80g) roasted pine nuts

creamy dressing
2 tablespoons olive oil
2 tablespoons white wine vinegar
2 teaspoons white balsamic vinegar
2 tablespoons coarsely chopped fresh basil leaves
¼ cup (60ml) cream

1 Make creamy dressing.

2 Place beans in large bowl with remaining ingredients and dressing; stir gently to combine.

creamy dressing Combine oil, vinegars and basil in small bowl. Add cream; whisk until combined.

prep time *15 minutes*   serves 4
nutritional count per serving *37.1g total fat (11g saturated fat); 1944kJ (465 cal); 13g carbohydrate; 17.1g protein; 7.7g fibre*

crispy polenta salad

bean salad with creamy dressing

We used a cryovac-packed ready-to-serve sweet chilli tofu in this recipe; there are various flavours of already marinated tofu pieces that can be found in the refrigerated section of most supermarkets and Asian food stores.

kaffir lime & rice salad with tofu & cashews

2 cups (400g) jasmine rice
2 fresh kaffir lime leaves, chopped finely
2 fresh long red chillies, chopped finely
2cm piece fresh ginger (10g), grated
400g packaged marinated tofu pieces, sliced thickly
½ cup coarsely chopped fresh coriander
1 large carrot (180g), cut into matchsticks
3 green onions, sliced thinly
¾ cup (120g) roasted unsalted cashews, chopped coarsely

lime & palm sugar dressing
1 teaspoon finely grated lime rind
½ cup (125ml) lime juice
2 tablespoons grated palm sugar
2 tablespoons fish sauce

1 Cook rice in large saucepan of boiling water, uncovered, until tender; drain. Rinse under cold water; drain.

2 Meanwhile, place ingredients for lime and palm sugar dressing in screw-top jar; shake well.

3 Place rice in large bowl with dressing, lime leaves, chilli, ginger, tofu, coriander, carrot, half the onion and ½ cup nuts; stir gently to combine. Serve salad sprinkled with remaining onion and nuts.

prep & cook time *30 minutes*   serves *4*
nutritional count per serving *22.2g total fat (3.7g saturated fat); 2847kJ (681 cal); 90.9g carbohydrate; 25.6g protein; 6.3g fibre*

kumara & rice salad

1 cup (200g) brown rice
1 small kumara (250g), chopped coarsely
250g red grape tomatoes, halved
2 green onions, sliced thinly
⅓ cup coarsely chopped fresh basil leaves
40g baby rocket leaves

balsamic dressing
2 tablespoons orange juice
1 tablespoon balsamic vinegar
1 teaspoon olive oil
1 clove garlic, crushed

1 Cook rice in large saucepan of boiling water, uncovered, about 30 minutes or until tender; drain. Rinse under cold water; drain.

2 Meanwhile, boil, steam or microwave kumara until tender; drain.

3 Place ingredients for balsamic dressing in screw-top jar; shake well.

4 Place rice and kumara in large bowl with remaining ingredients and dressing; toss gently to combine.

prep & cook time *40 minutes* serves *4*
nutritional count per serving *3g total fat (0.5g saturated fat); 1287kJ (308 cal); 60.3g carbohydrate; 6.9g protein; 5g fibre*

split pea salad with mustard dressing

½ cup (100g) yellow split peas
½ cup (100g) green split peas
4 green onions, sliced thinly
250g cherry tomatoes, halved
½ cup coarsely chopped fresh flat-leaf parsley

mustard dressing
¼ cup (60ml) lemon juice
¼ cup (60ml) olive oil
1 tablespoon wholegrain mustard
2 cloves garlic, crushed

1 Place peas in medium bowl, cover with cold water; stand overnight, drain. Rinse under cold water; drain.

2 Place peas in medium saucepan, cover with boiling water. Simmer, covered, about 10 minutes or until peas are tender; rinse under cold water, drain.

3 Whisk ingredients for mustard dressing in small bowl.

4 Combine peas in large bowl with remaining ingredients and dressing; mix gently.

prep & cook time *30 minutes (+ standing)* serves *6*
nutritional count per serving *9.9g total fat (1.4g saturated fat); 836kJ (200 cal); 17.3g carbohydrate; 8.3g protein; 4.7g fibre*

kumara & rice salad

split pea salad with mustard dressing

black bean, corn
& papaya salad

1 cup (200g) dried black beans
1 trimmed corn cob (250g)
5 medium egg tomatoes (375g), seeded
4 green onions, sliced thinly
1 cup (170g) diced papaya
⅓ cup coarsely chopped fresh coriander
4 large iceberg lettuce leaves

lime dressing
1 clove garlic, crushed
2 tablespoons lime juice
2 tablespoons olive oil
1 tablespoon white wine vinegar
½ teaspoon white sugar
1 fresh small red thai chilli, chopped finely

1 Cover beans with cold water in medium bowl; stand overnight, drain. Rinse beans under cold water; drain. Cook beans in medium saucepan of boiling water, uncovered, until beans are just tender. Drain.

2 Meanwhile, microwave, steam or grill corn until tender; cut kernels from cobs.

3 Blend or process tomato until just finely chopped.

4 Place ingredients for lime dressing in screw-top jar; shake well.

5 Place beans, corn and tomato in large bowl with onion, papaya, coriander and dressing; toss gently to combine. Divide salad among lettuce leaves.

prep & cook time *1 hour 15 minutes (+ standing)* serves 4
nutritional count per serving *9.9g total fat (1.4g saturated fat); 711kJ (170 cal); 13g carbohydrate; 4.4g protein; 5.4g fibre*

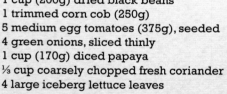

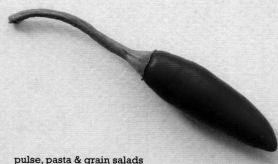

lentil, zucchini & chorizo salad

2 chorizo sausages (340g), sliced thinly
1 large zucchini (150g), sliced thinly lengthways
2 x 400g cans brown lentils, rinsed, drained
250g red grape tomatoes, halved
1 cup loosely packed fresh flat-leaf parsley leaves

cajun dressing
¼ cup (60ml) olive oil
1 tablespoon red wine vinegar
2 tablespoons cajun spice mix

1 Cook chorizo and zucchini on heated oiled grill plate (or grill or barbecue) until chorizo is cooked and zucchini is tender.

2 Meanwhile, place ingredients for cajun dressing in screw-top jar; shake well.

3 Place chorizo and zucchini in large bowl with dressing and reamaining ingredients; toss gently to combine.

prep & cook time *30 minutes* serves 4
nutritional count per serving *39.8g total fat (11.2g saturated fat); 2161kJ (517 cal); 13.9g carbohydrate; 24.1g protein; 6.2g fibre*

tuna, bean & haloumi salad

500g spinach, trimmed
250g haloumi cheese, cut lengthways into 1cm slices
2 x 420g cans four-bean mix, rinsed, drained
425g can tuna in oil, drained, flaked
250g yellow grape tomatoes, halved

creamy lemon dressing
½ cup (140g) greek-style yogurt
½ teaspoon finely grated lemon rind
1 teaspoon dijon mustard
¼ cup (60ml) lemon juice

1 Boil, steam or microwave spinach until wilted; drain, chop coarsely.

2 Meanwhile, combine ingredients for creamy lemon dressing in small bowl.

3 Cook cheese in heated oiled large frying pan until browned lightly.

4 Combine spinach, beans, tuna and tomato in large bowl. Divide salad among serving bowls; top with cheese, drizzle with dressing. Serve with lemon wedges, if you like.

prep & cook time *30 minutes* serves 4
nutritional count per serving *25.8g total fat (10.5g saturated fat); 2278kJ (545 cal); 25.6g carbohydrate; 47.1g protein; 11.4g fibre*

lentil, zucchini & chorizo salad

tuna, bean & haloumi salad

beetroot & lentil salad
with grilled pork sausages

1½ cups (350g) small brown lentils
2 sprigs fresh thyme
850g small beetroots, trimmed
1 tablespoon olive oil
1 large brown onion (200g), chopped finely
2 teaspoons yellow mustard seeds
2 teaspoons ground cumin
1 teaspoon ground coriander
½ cup (125ml) chicken stock
150g baby spinach leaves
8 thick pork sausages (960g)

thyme dressing
1 teaspoon fresh thyme
1 clove garlic, crushed
½ cup (125ml) red wine vinegar
¼ cup (60ml) olive oil

1 Place ingredients for thyme dressing in screw-top jar; shake well.

2 Cook lentils and thyme, uncovered, in large saucepan of boiling water until lentils are just tender; drain, discard thyme. Place lentils in large bowl with half of the dressing; toss gently to combine.

3 Meanwhile, discard any leaves and all but 2cm of the stalk from each beetroot. Boil, steam or microwave unpeeled beetroots until just tender; drain. When cool enough to handle, peel then quarter each beetroot; place in bowl with lentils.

4 Heat oil in large frying pan; cook onion, seeds and spices, stirring, until onion softens. Add stock; bring to the boil. Remove from heat; stir in spinach.

5 Place spinach mixture and remaining dressing in bowl with beetroot and lentil mixture; toss gently to combine.

6 Cook sausages in same cleaned pan until cooked through; serve sliced sausages with beetroot and lentil salad.

prep & cook time *1 hour* serves 4
nutritional count per serving *73.7g total fat (24.5g saturated fat); 4623kJ (1106 cal); 58.7g carbohydrate; 55.5g protein; 22.6g fibre*

risoni & broad bean salad

If you cannot buy fresh, use 500g frozen broad beans.

1kg fresh broad beans, shelled
250g risoni
1 tablespoon olive oil
3 green onions, sliced thinly
2 cloves garlic, sliced thinly
1 cup coarsely chopped fresh mint
¼ cup (60ml) lemon juice
500g cherry tomatoes, halved
1 tablespoon brown sugar
1 cup (80g) shaved parmesan cheese

1 Boil, steam or microwave beans until just tender; drain. Rinse under cold water; drain. Peel away grey-coloured outer shells.

2 Cook risoni in medium saucepan of boiling water, uncovered, until just tender; drain.

3 Meanwhile, heat oil in large frying pan; cook onion and garlic, stirring, until onion softens. Add risoni, beans, mint and juice; stir until combined. Transfer to large serving platter.

4 Cook tomato and sugar in same frying pan, stirring occasionally, about 5 minutes or until tomato just softens.

5 Top risoni salad with tomato; sprinkle with cheese.

prep & cook time *1 hour 15 minutes* serves *4*
nutritional count per serving *12.9g total fat (5.1g saturated fat); 1864kJ (446 cal); 53.3g carbohydrate; 27.5g protein; 15.8g fibre*

black bean & mango salad

1 cup (200g) dried black beans
1 lebanese cucumber (130g), seeded, sliced thinly
1 medium mango (430g), chopped finely
1 cup loosely packed fresh coriander leaves

sweet chilli dressing
1 tablespoon peanut oil
1 tablespoon sweet chilli sauce
1 tablespoon lime juice

1 Cover beans with cold water in medium bowl. Stand overnight; rinse, drain.

2 Cook beans in medium saucepan of boiling water until tender; drain.

3 Meanwhile, combine ingredients for sweet chilli dressing in small bowl.

4 Place beans in medium bowl with dressing and remaining ingredients; toss gently to combine.

prep & cook time *1 hour 40 minutes (+ standing)* serves *6*
nutritional count per serving *9.9g total fat (1.5g saturated fat); 790kJ (189 cal); 9.7g carbohydrate; 11.6g protein; 7.8g fibre*

risoni & broad bean salad

black bean & mango salad

cheesy polenta with tomato salad

bean salad with smoked salmon

pulse, pasta & grain salads

cheesy polenta with tomato salad

1 litre (4 cups) water
1 cup (170g) polenta
20g butter
1 cup (80g) finely grated parmesan cheese
200g red grape tomatoes, halved
200g yellow grape tomatoes, halved

salsa verde
½ cup finely chopped fresh flat-leaf parsley
¼ cup finely chopped fresh mint
¼ cup finely chopped fresh dill
¼ cup finely chopped fresh chives
1 tablespoon wholegrain mustard
2 tablespoons lemon juice
2 tablespoons drained capers, rinsed, chopped finely
1 clove garlic, crushed
⅓ cup (80ml) olive oil

1 Oil deep 19cm-square cake pan.

2 Place the water in large saucepan; bring to the boil. Gradually stir polenta into water; simmer, stirring, about 10 minutes or until polenta thickens, stir in butter and cheese. Spread polenta into pan; cool 10 minutes. Refrigerate about 1 hour or until firm.

3 Combine ingredients for salsa verde in small bowl.

4 Place tomatoes in medium bowl with a little of the salsa; stir gently to combine.

5 Turn polenta onto board; trim edges. Cut polenta into four squares; cut squares into two triangles. Cook polenta, both sides, in heated oiled grill pan until browned.

6 Serve polenta with tomato mixture and remaining salsa.

prep & cook time *50 minutes (+ refrigeration)* serves *4*
nutritional count per serving *29.9g total fat (9.5g saturated fat); 1902kJ (455 cal); 32.9g carbohydrate; 12.2g protein; 3.9g fibre*

bean salad with smoked salmon

500g frozen broad beans
400g can white beans, rinsed, drained
½ small red onion (50g), sliced thinly
1 lebanese cucumber (130g), chopped coarsely
1 teaspoon finely grated lemon rind
2 tablespoons lemon juice
1 tablespoon olive oil
300g smoked salmon

fried capers
¼ cup (50g) drained capers, rinsed
¼ cup (60ml) olive oil

1 Boil, steam or microwave broad beans until just tender. Peel; place in medium bowl. Add white beans, onion, cucumber, rind, juice and oil; toss gently to combine.

2 Meanwhile, make fried capers.

3 Arrange salmon slices on serving plates, top with fried capers; serve with bean salad and, if you like, lemon wedges.

fried capers Pat capers dry with absorbent paper. Heat oil in shallow small frying pan; add capers carefully (they will splatter), fry for about 2 minutes. Drain on absorbent paper.

prep & cook time *25 minutes* serves *4*
nutritional count per serving *22.2g total fat (3.2g saturated fat); 1705kJ (408 cal); 18.7g carbohydrate; 27.3g protein; 13.2g fibre*

warm split pea & sausage salad

1½ cups (300g) yellow split peas
2 rindless bacon rashers (130g), chopped coarsely
6 thin sausages (480g), chopped coarsely
1 medium carrot (120g), chopped coarsely
1 trimmed celery stalk (100g), chopped coarsely
1 medium brown onion (150g), chopped coarsely
2 cloves garlic, sliced thinly
250g grape tomatoes, halved
400g can white beans, rinsed, drained
2 teaspoons finely grated orange rind
⅓ cup (80ml) orange juice

1 Place peas in medium bowl, cover with cold water; stand overnight. Drain peas, rinse under cold water; drain.

2 Place peas in medium saucepan, cover with boiling water. Simmer, covered, about 10 minutes or until peas are tender; rinse under cold water, drain.

3 Meanwhile, cook bacon and sausage in large heated saucepan, in batches, until sausage is cooked.

4 Add carrot, celery, onion and garlic to pan; cook, stirring, until carrot softens slightly. Add tomatoes; cook, stirring, 2 minutes. Add beans, peas, bacon and sausage; stir to combine. Remove from heat; stir in rind and juice.

prep & cook time *40 minutes (+ standing)*   serves *4*
nutritional count per serving *33.9g total fat (15.1g saturated fat); 2985kJ (714 cal); 51.2g carbohydrate; 43g protein; 16.8g fibre*

pasta & garlic salad

500g farfalle pasta
¼ cup (60ml) olive oil
100g butter, chopped
2½ cups (175g) stale breadcrumbs
4 cloves garlic, crushed
1 cup coarsely chopped fresh flat-leaf parsley

1 Cook pasta in large saucepan of boiling water until tender; drain.

2 Meanwhile, heat oil and butter in large frying pan; cook breadcrumbs and garlic over medium heat, stirring, until breadcrumbs brown.

3 Place hot pasta, breadcrumbs and parsley in large bowl; toss gently to combine.

prep & cook time *20 minutes*   serves *6*
nutritional count per serving *24.8g total fat (10.7g saturated fat); 2483kJ (594 cal); 76.4g carbohydrate; 13.7g protein; 4.8g fibre*

creamy tomato pasta salad

500g rigatoni pasta
10 slices prosciutto (150g)
1 cup (240g) crème fraîche
½ cup (160g) tomato chutney
300g cherry bocconcini cheese, halved
1 small red onion (100g), sliced thinly
1 cup loosely packed fresh basil leaves, chopped coarsely

1 Cook pasta in large saucepan of boiling water until tender; drain. Rinse under cold water; drain.

2 Meanwhile, cook prosciutto in heated oiled large frying pan until crisp. Drain on absorbent paper; chop coarsely.

3 Combine crème fraîche and chutney in large bowl, then add pasta, prosciutto and remaining ingredients; toss gently to combine.

prep & cook time *25 minutes*   serves *6*
nutritional count per serving *26g total fat (16.1g saturated fat); 2592kJ (620 cal); 70.6g carbohydrate; 23.9g protein; 3.7g fibre*

pasta & garlic salad

creamy tomato pasta salad

mexican bean salad with tortilla chips

4 medium tomatoes (600g), seeded, chopped coarsely
420g can four-bean mix, rinsed, drained
300g can kidney beans, rinsed, drained
½ cup coarsely chopped fresh coriander
¼ cup (60ml) lime juice
1 small red onion (100g), chopped finely
2 fresh long red chillies, chopped finely
4 small flour tortillas, cut into wedges
1 small avocado (200g)
2 tablespoons light sour cream

1 Preheat oven to 200°C/180°C fan-forced.

2 Combine tomato, beans, ⅓ cup of the coriander,
1 tablespoon of the juice, half of the onion and half of
the chilli in medium bowl.

3 Place tortilla wedges, in single layer, on oven tray;
toast about 5 minutes or until crisp.

4 Meanwhile, to make guacamole, mash avocado in small
bowl; stir in remaining coriander, juice, onion and chilli.

5 Divide tortilla chips among plates; top with bean mixture,
guacamole and sour cream.

prep & cook time *25 minutes* serves *4*
nutritional count per serving *14g total fat (3.7g saturated fat);
1522kJ (364 cal); 44.9g carbohydrate; 14.1g protein; 10.9g fibre*

chicken & pasta salad

pasta salad with brussels sprouts

pulse, pasta & grain salads

chicken & pasta salad

375g large shell pasta
1 cup (120g) frozen peas
3 cups (480g) shredded barbecued chicken
40g baby rocket leaves

rocket pesto
40g baby rocket leaves
2 tablespoons roasted pine nuts
½ cup (40g) finely grated parmesan cheese
2 teaspoons finely grated lemon rind
1 tablespoon lemon juice
¼ cup (60ml) olive oil

1 Cook pasta in large saucepan of boiling water until tender. Add peas during last 2 minutes of pasta cooking time; drain.

2 Meanwhile, make rocket pesto.

3 Place pasta, peas and rocket pesto in large bowl with remaining ingredients; toss gently to combine.

rocket pesto Blend or process rocket, nuts, cheese, rind and juice until finely chopped. With motor operating, gradually add oil in a thin steady stream; blend until pesto is smooth.

prep & cook time *30 minutes* serves *4*
nutritional count per serving *32.4g total fat (7.1g saturated fat); 3168kJ (758 cal); 66.6g carbohydrate; 47g protein; 5.6g fibre*

pasta salad with brussels sprouts

500g rigatoni pasta
1 tablespoon olive oil
300g brussels sprouts, trimmed, shredded
½ cup coarsely chopped fresh flat-leaf parsley
1 tablespoon drained capers, rinsed
200g bocconcini cheese, sliced thickly
½ cup (80g) roasted almonds, chopped coarsely

red wine vinaigrette
⅓ cup (80ml) lemon juice
⅓ cup (80ml) red wine vinegar
¼ cup (60ml) olive oil
1 teaspoon white sugar
2 cloves garlic, crushed

1 Place ingredients for red wine vinaigrette in screw-top jar; shake well.

2 Cook pasta in large saucepan of boiling water, uncovered, until just tender; drain.

3 Heat oil in same pan; stir-fry sprouts about 1 minute or until just warm.

4 Place pasta and sprouts in large serving bowl with remaining ingredients and vinaigrette; toss gently to combine.

prep & cook time *35 minutes* serves *4*
nutritional count per serving *25.7g total fat (5.7g saturated fat); 2358kJ (564 cal); 60g carbohydrate; 19.9g protein; 6.2g fibre*

cheese & egg salads

bocconcini salad with tomato pesto, page 118

Cheese and egg salads are among the
most familiar and best-loved in the world.
And now that once-esoteric cheeses can be
found in our supermarkets there's a greater
variety of exotic salads to create.

117

bocconcini salad with tomato pesto

270g jar semi-dried tomatoes in oil
¼ cup (20g) coarsely grated parmesan cheese
1 tablespoon roasted pine nuts
1 fresh long red chilli, chopped coarsely
2 tablespoons lemon juice
⅓ cup (80ml) cream
630g cherry bocconcini cheese, drained
1 cup (150g) plain flour
2 eggs, beaten lightly
1 cup (100g) packaged breadcrumbs
vegetable oil, for deep-frying
4 white witlof (500g), trimmed
¼ cup mizuna

1   Drain tomatoes over small bowl; reserve ½ cup of the oil. Roughly chop half the tomatoes; slice remaining tomatoes into thin strips.

2   Blend chopped tomatoes, parmesan, nuts, chilli and juice until smooth. With motor operating, gradually add reserved oil in a thin, steady stream; blend until smooth. Transfer pesto to small jug; stir in cream.

3   Coat bocconcini in flour; shake off excess. Dip in egg, then coat in breadcrumbs.

4   Heat oil in medium deep saucepan; deep-fry bocconcini, in batches, until browned lightly. Drain on absorbent paper.

5   Divide witlof among serving plates; top with bocconcini then sprinkle with sliced tomato and mizuna. Drizzle over pesto to serve.

prep & cook time *45 minutes*   serves *4*
nutritional count per serving *52.5g total fat (25.1g saturated fat); 3867kJ (925 cal); 60.7g carbohydrate; 47g protein; 11.5g fibre*

pumpkin, ricotta & beetroot salad

4 baby beetroot (100g)
800g pumpkin, unpeeled, cut into 8 wedges
2 tablespoons olive oil
40g mesclun
1 cup (120g) coarsely chopped roasted pecans
200g ricotta cheese, crumbled

lemon myrtle dressing
1 tablespoon cider vinegar
1 tablespoon lemon juice
1 teaspoon ground lemon myrtle
2 tablespoons olive oil

1   Preheat oven to 200°C/180°C fan-forced.

2   Remove unblemished leaves from beetroot, reserve. Peel and halve beetroot.

3   Combine beetroot, pumpkin and oil in large shallow baking dish. Roast, uncovered, turning occasionally, about 40 minutes or until vegetables are tender.

4   Meanwhile, place ingredients for lemon myrtle dressing in screw-top jar; shake well.

5   Combine vegetables, beetroot leaves, mesclun, nuts and cheese in large bowl; drizzle with dressing.

prep & cook time *55 minutes*   serves *4*
nutritional count per serving *37.5g total fat (6.8g saturated fat); 1885kJ (451 cal); 14.7g carbohydrate; 12.2g protein; 3.4g fibre*

Ground lemon myrtle is available from specialist spice shops and some gourmet food stores. Lemon myrtle is a small tree that grows in sub-tropical and tropical rainforest areas of Queensland. Ground lemon myrtle is a ground mixture of the dried leaf and flower; it has a strong lemon flavour. If you can't find it, use 1 teaspoon finely grated lemon rind instead.

pumpkin, ricotta & beetroot salad

duck, blue cheese & pear salad

4 duck breast fillets (600g), skin on
1 small red oak leaf lettuce, trimmed
2 witlof (250g), trimmed
1 medium pear (230g), halved, cored, sliced thinly
1 cup (100g) roasted walnuts
150g soft blue cheese, crumbled

red wine vinaigrette
¼ cup (60ml) olive oil
¼ cup (60ml) red wine vinegar
2 teaspoons wholegrain mustard

1 Cook duck, skin-side down, in heated large frying pan about 5 minutes or until skin is browned and crisp. Turn duck; cook about 5 minutes or until cooked as desired. Drain on absorbent paper; slice thinly.

2 Meanwhile, place ingredients for red wine vinaigrette in screw-top jar; shake well.

3 Place duck in large bowl with lettuce, witlof, pear and nuts; toss gently to combine. Drizzle with vinaigrette, sprinkle with cheese.

prep & cook time *25 minutes* serves *4*
nutritional count per serving *99g total fat (27.5g saturated fat); 4431kJ (1060 cal); 8.8g carbohydrate; 33.1g protein; 6.5g fibre*

ricotta & broad bean salad

500g frozen broad beans
340g asparagus, trimmed, halved crossways
450g can whole baby beetroot, drained, quartered
½ cup loosely packed fresh flat-leaf parsley leaves
½ cup loosely packed fresh mint leaves
80g low-fat ricotta cheese, crumbled

hazelnut oil dressing
1 tablespoon white wine vinegar
1 teaspoon hazelnut oil
½ teaspoon white sugar

1 Cook broad beans in large saucepan of boiling water about 3 minutes or until tender, drain; rinse under cold water, drain.

2 Boil, steam or microwave asparagus until almost tender, drain; rinse under cold water, drain.

3 Place ingredients for hazelnut oil dressing in screw-top jar; shake well.

4 Place beans and asparagus in large bowl with beetroot, parsley and mint; toss gently to combine. Serve topped with cheese; drizzle with dressing.

prep & cook time *30 minutes* serves *4*
nutritional count per serving *3.5g total fat (1.2g saturated fat); 732kJ (175 cal); 18.5g carbohydrate; 11g protein; 13g fibre*

duck, blue cheese & pear salad

ricotta & broad bean salad

grilled goats cheese salad

1 small french bread stick (150g), sliced thinly
2 tablespoons olive oil
½ cup (50g) roasted walnuts, coarsely chopped
⅓ cup coarsely chopped fresh flat-leaf parsley
1 clove garlic, chopped finely
2 tablespoons walnut oil
1 tablespoon white wine vinegar
300g log goats cheese, cut into 4 slices
80g mesclun

1 Brush bread with olive oil; cook on heated oiled grill plate (or grill or barbecue) until browned both sides.

2 Meanwhile, combine nuts, parsley, garlic, walnut oil and vinegar in small bowl.

3 Preheat grill. Place cheese slices on oven tray; cook, under grill, until browned lightly.

4 Divide mesclun among serving plates; top with cheese and walnut mixture, serve with bread.

prep & cook time *20 minutes*   serves 4
nutritional count per serving *34.4g total fat (10.2g saturated fat); 1952kJ (467 cal); 21.8g carbohydrate; 16.6g protein; 3.5g fibre*

goats cheese & fig salad

haloumi & chicken salad

cheese & egg salads

goats cheese & fig salad

6 slices prosciutto (90g)
120g baby rocket leaves, trimmed
4 large fresh figs (320g), quartered
150g soft goats cheese, crumbled

honey cider dressing
¼ cup (60ml) cider vinegar
2 tablespoons olive oil
1 tablespoon wholegrain mustard
1 tablespoon honey

1 Preheat grill.

2 Place ingredients for honey cider dressing in screw-top jar; shake well.

3 Crisp prosciutto under grill; drain, chop coarsely.

4 Serve rocket topped with fig, cheese and prosciutto; drizzle with dressing.

prep & cook time *15 minutes* **serves** *4*
nutritional count per serving *16.9g total fat (5.7g saturated fat); 1062kJ (254 cal); 13.7g carbohydrate; 11.1g protein; 2.6g fibre*

haloumi & chicken salad

2 tablespoons olive oil
1 tablespoon balsamic vinegar
2 cloves garlic, crushed
1 tablespoon coarsely chopped fresh rosemary
800g chicken thigh fillets
600g piece pumpkin, trimmed, sliced thinly
300g asparagus, trimmed
2 x 180g packets haloumi cheese
250g rocket, trimmed

rosemary balsamic dressing
2 tablespoons olive oil
1 tablespoon balsamic vinegar
1 tablespoon lemon juice
1 tablespoon coarsely chopped fresh rosemary leaves

1 Place ingredients for rosemary balsamic dressing in screw-top jar; shake well.

2 Combine oil, vinegar, garlic, rosemary and chicken in medium bowl. Cook chicken on heated oiled grill plate (or grill or barbecue); cover.

3 Cook pumpkin and asparagus, in batches, on grill plate until tender. Transfer to large bowl; cover.

4 Slice cheese thickly; cook on cleaned grill plate until browned both sides.

5 Slice chicken thickly. Add cheese, rocket and dressing to bowl with pumpkin and asparagus; toss gently to combine.

prep & cook time *50 minutes* **serves** *4*
nutritional count per serving *49.1g total fat (17.2g saturated fat); 3106kJ (743 cal); 12.2g carbohydrate; 62.6g protein; 3.8g fibre*

lentil & goats cheese salad

1 medium red capsicum (200g), sliced thickly
2 tablespoons extra virgin olive oil
½ cup (110g) puy lentils, rinsed, drained
1 medium brown onion (150g), halved
1 bay leaf
16 sprigs fresh thyme
300g piece firm goats cheese
2 tablespoons packaged breadcrumbs
2 teaspoons finely grated lemon rind
1 tablespoon coarsely chopped fresh flat-leaf parsley
250g cherry tomatoes, halved
100g mesclun

vinaigrette
1 tablespoon red wine vinegar
2 tablespoons extra virgin olive oil
1 teaspoon dijon mustard
1 teaspoon sugar

1 Preheat oven to 240°C/220°C fan-forced.

2 Combine capsicum and half of the oil in large shallow baking dish. Roast, uncovered, about 15 minutes or until capsicum just softens.

3 Meanwhile, combine lentils, onion, bay leaf and thyme in medium saucepan, cover with water; bring to the boil. Reduce heat; simmer, covered, about 20 minutes or until lentils just tender. Drain; discard onion, bay leaf and thyme.

4 Meanwhile, place ingredients for vinaigrette in screw-top jar; shake well.

5 Cut cheese into 16 pieces; coat cheese in breadcrumbs. Heat remaining oil in medium frying pan; cook cheese, uncovered, about 5 minutes or until cheese is browned lightly all over and starting to melt.

6 Meanwhile, combine lentils in medium bowl with rind, parsley, tomato and two-thirds of the vinaigrette. Divide lentils among serving plates; top with capsicum, mesclun then cheese, drizzle with remaining vinaigrette.

prep & cook time *1 hour 10 minutes*   serves *4*
nutritional count per serving *30.5g total fat (10.4g saturated fat); 1555kJ (372 cal); 10.6g carbohydrate; 13.3g protein; 3.3g fibre*

root vegetable salad with lemon & fetta

500g baby new potatoes, unpeeled, halved
500g butternut pumpkin, chopped coarsely
4 small beetroot (400g), peeled
1 medium parsnip (250g), quartered
400g baby carrots, trimmed
1 medium lemon (140g), sliced thinly
2 tablespoons olive oil
30g butter, chopped
2 tablespoons fresh oregano leaves
2 tablespoons lemon juice
1 tablespoon wholegrain mustard
100g baby rocket leaves
100g fetta cheese, crumbled

1   Preheat oven to 200°C/180°C fan-forced.

2   Combine potato, pumpkin, beetroot, parsnip, carrots, lemon, oil, butter and half the oregano in large shallow baking dish. Roast, uncovered, turning occasionally, about 40 minutes or until vegetables are tender.

3   Meanwhile, place juice and mustard in screw-top jar; shake well.

4   Place vegetables in large bowl with mustard mixture and rocket; toss gently to combine. Sprinkle over cheese and remaining oregano leaves.

prep & cook time *50 minutes*   serves *4*
nutritional count per serving   *22.2g total fat (9.5g saturated fat); 1881kJ (450 cal); 42.6g carbohydrate; 14g protein; 12.2g fibre*

eggplant, fetta & semi-dried tomato salad

2 medium red capsicums (400g)
8 baby eggplants (480g), halved lengthways
1 medium red onion (170g), cut into wedges
250g fetta cheese, crumbled
350g watercress, trimmed
100g drained semi-dried tomatoes, sliced thinly

creamy horseradish dressing
1 egg
2 teaspoons honey
2 tablespoons prepared horseradish
2 cloves garlic, quartered
⅔ cup (160ml) olive oil

1   Quarter capsicums; discard seeds and membranes. Cook capsicum, eggplant and onion, in batches, on heated oiled grill plate (or grill or barbecue) until browned. Cover capsicum pieces for 5 minutes; peel.

2   Make creamy horseradish dressing.

3   Combine cheese, watercress and tomato in medium bowl; divide among serving plates. Top with capsicum, eggplant and onion; drizzle with dressing.

creamy horseradish dressing Blend or process egg, honey, horseradish and garlic until smooth. With motor operating, add oil in thin, steady stream until dressing thickens slightly.

prep & cook time *35 minutes*   serves *6*
nutritional count per serving   *36.3g total fat (10.2g saturated fat); 1910kJ (457 cal); 14.6g carbohydrate; 15.1g protein; 8.2g fibre*

root vegetable salad with lemon & fetta

eggplant, fetta & semi-dried tomato salad

egg & bacon salad

1 medium kumara (400g), cut into 2cm pieces
cooking-oil spray
4 rindless bacon rashers (260g)
6 hard-boiled eggs, quartered
1 stalk celery (150g), trimmed, sliced thinly
80g mesclun

honey mustard dressing
½ cup (140g) mayonnaise
¼ cup (60ml) cider vinegar
1 tablespoon honey
2 teaspoons wholegrain mustard

1 Preheat oven to 220°C/200°C fan-forced.

2 Place kumara on oven tray; spray with cooking oil.
Roast, uncovered, about 20 minutes or until tender.

3 Meanwhile, cook bacon in heated large frying pan;
drain on absorbent paper. Chop coarsely.

4 Combine ingredients for honey mustard dressing in
small bowl.

5 Place kumara and bacon in large bowl with remaining
ingredients and dressing; toss gently to combine.

prep & cook time *25 minutes* serves 4
nutritional count per serving *29.2g total fat (6.9g saturated
fat); 1965kJ (470 cal); 25.9g carbohydrate; 25g protein;
2.6g fibre*

haloumi, prosciutto & spinach salad

13 slices prosciutto (200g)
500g asparagus, trimmed
200g haloumi cheese, sliced thinly
2 small pears (360g), cored, cut into thin wedges
200g baby spinach leaves

macadamia dressing
½ cup (75g) roasted macadamias, chopped coarsely
2 tablespoons sherry vinegar
¼ cup (60ml) macadamia oil

1 Preheat grill.

2 Cook prosciutto under preheated grill until crisp; break prosciutto into bite-size pieces.

3 Meanwhile, boil, steam or microwave asparagus until just tender; drain.

4 Place ingredients for macadamia dressing in screw-top jar; shake well.

5 Cook asparagus, cheese and pear on heated oiled grill plate (or grill or barbecue) until browned lightly.

6 Place prosciutto and asparagus in large bowl with cheese, pear, spinach and dressing; toss gently to combine.

prep & cook time *35 minutes* serves *4*
nutritional count per serving *39.9g total fat (10.5g saturated fat); 2182kJ (522 cal); 14.8g carbohydrate; 24.7g protein; 5.3g fibre*

shaved fennel & apple salad with brie & pecans

2 baby fennel (260g)
2 medium green apples (300g)
1 cup (120g) roasted pecans, halved lengthways
150g brie cheese, sliced thinly into wedges
1 red coral lettuce, trimmed, chopped coarsely

mustard vinaigrette
⅓ cup (80ml) olive oil
¼ cup (60ml) lemon juice
1 tablespoon wholegrain mustard

1 Place ingredients for mustard vinaigrette in screw-top jar; shake well.

2 Trim fennel; reserve 2 tablespoons coarsely chopped frond-tips. Halve and core unpeeled apples. Using a sharp knife, mandoline or V-slicer, slice fennel and apple thinly.

3 Place fennel and apple in large bowl with frond tips, nuts, cheese and dressing; toss gently to combine. Serve salad on top of lettuce.

prep time *20 minutes* serves *6*
nutritional count per serving *33.3g total fat (6.8g saturated fat); 1496kJ (358 cal); 6.6g carbohydrate; 7.4g protein; 3.5g fibre*

potato, tuna & egg salad

6 baby new potatoes (240g)
100g green beans, trimmed, halved crossways
2 tablespoons skim-milk natural yogurt
1 teaspoon finely grated lemon rind
2 teaspoons lemon juice
185g can tuna in springwater, drained, flaked
3 green onions, sliced finely
1 tablespoon coarsely chopped fresh flat-leaf parsley
2 hard-boiled eggs, quartered

1 Boil, steam or microwave potatoes and beans, separately, until tender; drain, cool.

2 Meanwhile, combine yogurt, rind and juice in medium bowl.

3 Quarter potatoes; add to yogurt mixture with tuna, onion and parsley, stir to combine. Serve salad topped with egg.

prep & cook time *20 minutes*   serves *2*
nutritional count per serving *2.5g total fat (2.4g saturated fat); 1150kJ (275 cal); 18.9g carbohydrate; 30.7g protein; 3.9g fibre*

ricotta & zucchini pasta salad

500g penne pasta
4 large zucchini (600g), sliced thinly lengthways
⅓ cup (80ml) olive oil
1 tablespoon finely grated lemon rind
⅓ cup (80ml) lemon juice
2 cloves garlic, crushed
400g ricotta cheese, crumbled
½ cup loosely packed fresh basil leaves, shredded finely

1 Cook pasta in large saucepan of boiling water until tender; drain.

2 Meanwhile, combine zucchini and half the oil in medium bowl. Cook zucchini, in batches, on heated oiled grill plate (or grill or barbecue) until tender.

3 Combine zucchini, rind, juice, garlic and remaining oil in large bowl. Add pasta, cheese and basil; toss gently to combine.

prep & cook time *25 minutes*   serves *6*
nutritional count per serving *21g total fat (6.7g saturated fat); 2128kJ (509 cal); 59.8g carbohydrate; 17.7g protein; 4.7g fibre*

potato, tuna & egg salad

ricotta & zucchini pasta salad

char-grilled vegetable & bocconcini stack with basil sauce

4 large red capsicums (1.4kg)
4 flat mushrooms (320g)
6 baby eggplants (360g), halved lengthways
150g mesclun
14 bocconcini cheese (420g), sliced thickly

lemon oil
1 teaspoon finely grated lemon rind
2 tablespoons lemon juice
2 tablespoons olive oil

basil dressing
2 tablespoons red wine vinegar
1 tablespoon wholegrain mustard
1 cup firmly packed fresh basil leaves
1 tablespoon water
¼ cup (60ml) olive oil

1 Make lemon oil. Make basil dressing.

2 Quarter capsicums; discard seeds and membranes. Roast under grill or in very hot oven, skin-side up, until skin blisters and blackens. Cover capsicum pieces with plastic or paper for 5 minutes; peel away skin then cut into thick slices.

3 Meanwhile, cook mushrooms and eggplant, in batches, on heated oiled grill plate (or grill or barbecue) until browned all over.

4 Place mesclun in large bowl with lemon oil; toss gently to combine.

5 Divide mesclun among serving plates, top with mushrooms, eggplant, cheese and capsicum; drizzle with dressing.

lemon oil Place ingredients in screw-top jar; shake well.

basil dressing Blend or process ingredients until smooth.

prep & cook time *1 hour 10 minutes* serves *4*
nutritional count per serving *40g total fat (13.7g saturated fat); 2274kJ (544 cal); 15.3g carbohydrate; 27.6 protein; 8.7g fibre*

asparagus & spinach salad

340g asparagus, trimmed
4 eggs
200g baby spinach leaves, trimmed
¼ cup (20g) flaked pecorino cheese

dill lemon dressing
¼ cup (75g) mayonnaise
1 tablespoon lemon juice
1 tablespoon water
2 tablespoons finely chopped fresh dill

1 Place ingredients for dill lemon dressing in screw-top jar; shake well.

2 Cook asparagus, in batches, on heated oiled grill plate (or grill or barbecue); chop coarsely.

3 Half-fill a large shallow frying pan with water; bring to the boil. One at a time, break eggs into cup and slide into pan. When all eggs are in pan, allow water to return to the boil. Cover pan, turn off heat; stand about 4 minutes or until a light film of egg white sets over yolks. One at a time, remove eggs, using slotted spoon, and place on absorbent-paper-lined saucer to blot poaching liquid.

4 Divide spinach and asparagus among serving plates; top with an egg and a quarter of the cheese then drizzle spinach and asparagus with dressing.

prep & cook time *15 minutes* serves *4*
nutritional count per serving *12.9g total fat (3.1g saturated fat); 782kJ (187 cal); 5.4g carbohydrate; 11.6g protein; 2.7g fibre*

spinach, speck & egg salad

300g speck, sliced thinly
200g baby spinach leaves
¼ cup coarsely chopped fresh basil
50g pecorino cheese, shaved
4 eggs

garlic vinaigrette
2 cloves garlic, crushed
1 teaspoon dijon mustard
⅓ cup (80ml) extra virgin olive oil
¼ cup (60ml) balsamic vinegar

1 Cook speck in large non-stick frying pan, stirring occasionally, until crisp. Drain on absorbent paper; cool.

2 Meanwhile, place ingredients for garlic vinaigrette in screw-top jar; shake well.

3 Place speck in medium bowl with spinach, basil and cheese; toss gently to combine.

4 Half-fill a large shallow frying pan with water; bring to the boil. One at a time, break eggs into cup and slide into pan. When all eggs are in pan, allow water to return to the boil. Cover pan, turn off heat; stand about 4 minutes or until a light film of egg white sets over yolks. One at a time, remove eggs, using slotted spoon, and place on absorbent-paper-lined saucer to blot poaching liquid.

5 Divide salad among serving plates; top each with an egg then drizzle with vinaigrette.

prep & cook time *30 minutes* serves *4*
nutritional count per serving *37.6g total fat (10.5g saturated fat); 1898kJ (454 cal); 0.7g carbohydrate; 28.5g protein; 1.7g fibre*

asparagus & spinach salad

spinach, speck & egg salad

Young pencil leeks, about a quarter of the size of normal mature leeks, are so sweet and tender they can be steamed or braised and eaten like asparagus.

braised leek, kipfler & witlof salad with poached eggs

1kg kipfler potatoes, halved lengthways
2 teaspoons sea salt
½ teaspoon cracked black pepper
2 cloves garlic, crushed
olive oil cooking-spray
1 tablespoon olive oil
20 pencil leeks (1.6kg), trimmed to 15cm in length
6 white witlof (750g), halved lengthways
⅔ cup (160ml) dry white wine
1 cup (250ml) vegetable stock
1 teaspoon sugar
8 eggs

creamy chervil dressing
2 tablespoons lemon juice
1 tablespoon wholegrain mustard
⅔ cup (160ml) cream
¼ cup loosely packed fresh chervil leaves

1   Preheat oven to 200°C/180°C fan-forced.

2   Place ingredients for creamy chervil dressing in screw-top jar; shake well.

3   Toss potato with salt, pepper and garlic in large baking dish; spray lightly with cooking-oil spray. Roast, uncovered, about 50 minutes or until tender and crisp.

4   Meanwhile, heat oil in large flameproof baking dish; cook leeks and witlof, cut-side down, in single layer, for 1 minute. Add wine, stock and sugar; bring to the boil. Reduce heat; simmer, uncovered, 2 minutes. Cover tightly; transfer dish to oven for last 20 minutes of potato cooking time.

5   With 10 minutes left of potato cooking time, half-fill a large shallow frying pan with water; bring to the boil. One at a time, break eggs into cup and slide into pan. When all eggs are in pan, allow water to return to the boil. Cover pan, turn off heat; stand about 4 minutes or until a light film of egg white sets over yolks. One at a time, remove eggs, using slotted spoon, and place on absorbent-paper-lined saucer to blot poaching liquid.

6   Divide potato and witlof among serving plates; top with leeks and 2 eggs each, drizzle with dressing.

prep & cook time *1 hour 10 minutes*   serves *4*
nutritional count per serving *35.5g total fat (15.6g saturated fat); 2847kJ (681 cal); 47.9g carbohydrate; 28.5g protein; 16.6g fibre*

curried egg salad

egg & asparagus salad

curried egg salad

1 stalk celery (150g), trimmed, cut into matchsticks
¼ small red onion (25g), sliced thinly
½ cup coarsely chopped fresh flat-leaf parsley
4 hard-boiled eggs, grated finely
4 small butter lettuce leaves, chopped

curry mayonnaise
⅓ cup (100g) mayonnaise
1 tablespoon lemon juice
½ teaspoon curry powder

1 Combine ingredients for curry mayonnaise in small bowl.

2 Combine celery, onion and parsley in medium bowl.

3 Spread lettuce on serving plates, top with egg then celery mixture; drizzle with mayonnaise.

prep time *20 minutes* serves *4*
nutritional count per serving *15.2g total fat (3g saturated fat); 832kJ (199 cal); 6.1g carbohydrate; 9.3g protein; 1.2g fibre*

egg & asparagus salad

500g asparagus, trimmed, halved
½ cup (55g) coarsely chopped roasted walnuts
½ cup (40g) coarsely grated parmesan cheese
250g yellow teardrop tomatoes, halved
8 eggs
1 small french bread stick (150g), sliced thinly

lime, garlic and dill dressing
¼ cup (60ml) olive oil
2 teaspoons finely grated lime rind
1 tablespoon lime juice
1 clove garlic, crushed
2 teaspoons finely chopped fresh dill

1 Place ingredients for lime, garlic and dill dressing in screw-top jar; shake well.

2 Boil, steam or microwave asparagus until tender; drain. Combine asparagus, nuts, cheese, tomato and dressing in medium bowl. Divide asparagus mixture among serving plates.

3 Half-fill a large shallow frying pan with water; bring to the boil. One at a time, break eggs into cup and slide into pan. When all eggs are in pan, allow water to return to the boil. Cover pan, turn off heat; stand about 4 minutes or until a light film of egg white sets over yolks. One at a time, remove eggs, using slotted spoon, and place on absorbent-paper-lined saucer to blot poaching liquid. Toast bread.

4 Top salad with eggs, serve with toast.

prep & cook time *20 minutes* serves *4*
nutritional count per serving *38.5g total fat (8g saturated fat); 2282kJ (546 cal); 23.4g carbohydrate; 25.1g protein; 4.8g fibre*

asian salads

vietnamese beef salad, page 148

If you're new to Asian salads you're in for a pleasant surprise. Green mango and papaya, noodles and fresh herbs are common ingredients, along with beef, pork, chicken and prawns.

147

vietnamese beef salad

400g beef fillet, sliced thinly
2 teaspoons finely grated lime rind
¼ cup (60ml) lime juice
1 tablespoon fish sauce
1 tablespoon grated palm sugar
1 clove garlic, crushed
10cm stick lemon grass (20g), crushed, chopped finely
1 fresh small red thai chilli, chopped finely
2cm piece fresh ginger (10g), grated
¼ cup (60ml) peanut oil
1 cup (80g) bean sprouts
1 medium red capsicum (200g), sliced thinly
1 medium carrot (120g), cut into matchsticks
1 cup loosely packed vietnamese mint leaves
1 cup loosely packed fresh coriander leaves

1 Combine beef, rind, juice, sauce, sugar, garlic, lemon grass, chilli, ginger and 2 tablespoons of the oil in medium bowl; refrigerate 1 hour.

2 Heat remaining oil in wok; stir-fry beef mixture, in batches, until browned.

3 Place beef in large bowl with remaining ingredients; toss gently to combine.

prep & cook time *25 minutes (+ refrigeration)* serves *4*
nutritional count per serving *20g total fat (5g saturated fat); 1325kJ (317 cal); 8.7g carbohydrate; 24.1g protein; 3.6g fibre*

thai beef salad with chilli & lime

500g beef fillet, trimmed
100g rice vermicelli noodles
1 lebanese cucumber (130g), seeded, sliced thinly
½ cup firmly packed fresh coriander leaves
⅓ cup firmly packed fresh thai basil leaves
10cm stick lemon grass (20g), crushed, sliced thinly
2 fresh kaffir lime leaves, shredded finely
2 shallots (50g), sliced thinly
2 tablespoons fried shallots

thai dressing
2 fresh small red thai chillies, halved
1 clove garlic, quartered
¼ teaspoon caster sugar
⅓ cup (80ml) lime juice
2 tablespoons fish sauce

1 Cook beef on heated oiled grill plate (or grill or barbecue) until cooked as desired. Cover beef; stand 5 minutes then slice thinly.

2 Meanwhile, place noodles in medium heatproof bowl, cover with boiling water; stand until tender, drain. Rinse under cold water; drain.

3 Make thai dressing.

4 Place beef and noodles in large bowl with cucumber, herbs, lemon grass, lime leaves and sliced shallot; toss gently to combine.

5 Divide salad among serving plates; drizzle with dressing, sprinkle with fried shallots.

thai dressing Using mortar and pestle, crush chilli, garlic and sugar to a paste. Combine paste with remaining ingredients in small bowl.

prep & cook time *30 minutes* serves *4*
nutritional count per serving *8.3g total fat (3.2g saturated fat); 1133kJ (271 cal); 18.6g carbohydrate; 29.5g protein; 1.5g fibre*

thai beef salad with chilli & lime

salt & pepper squid salad

600g cleaned squid hoods
¼ cup (35g) plain flour
1 fresh long red chilli, chopped finely
1 teaspoon sea salt flakes
½ teaspoon cracked black pepper
vegetable oil, for deep-frying
50g mesclun
1 small red capsicum (150g), sliced thinly
1 lebanese cucumber (130g), sliced thinly
⅓ cup loosely packed fresh coriander leaves
2 teaspoons olive oil
1 medium lemon (140g), cut into wedges

1   Cut squid down centre to open out; score the inside
in a diagonal pattern. Halve squid lengthways; cut each
piece in half crossways.

2   Combine flour, chilli, salt and pepper in medium bowl;
add squid, toss to coat in flour mixture. Shake away excess.

3   Heat vegetable oil in wok; deep-fry squid, in batches,
until tender. Drain.

4   Place mesclun, capsicum, cucumber, coriander and
olive oil in large bowl with warm squid. Serve with lemon.

prep & cook time *45 minutes*   serves *4*
nutritional count per serving *12.6g total fat (2g
saturated fat); 1112kJ (266 cal); 9g carbohydrate;
27g protein; 2.3g fibre*

garlic prawns & tat soi salad

4 x 9cm-square wonton wrappers
1kg uncooked medium king prawns
4 cloves garlic, crushed
2 teaspoons olive oil
80g tat soi leaves
1 fresh long red chilli, cut into matchsticks

ginger soy dressing
¼ cup (60ml) peanut oil
1 teaspoon sesame oil
2 tablespoons lime juice
1 tablespoon light soy sauce
1cm piece fresh ginger (5g), grated

1   Preheat oven to 200°C/180°C fan-forced. Oil and line two
oven trays.

2   Place wonton wrappers on trays; bake about 5 minutes or
until crisp.

3   Place ingredients for ginger soy dressing in screw-top jar;
shake well.

4   Shell and devein prawns, leaving tails intact; combine
prawns and garlic in medium bowl. Heat oil in large frying pan;
cook prawns until changed in colour.

5   Combine tat soi, chilli and half the dressing in large bowl.

6   Divide salad among serving plates; top with prawns,
drizzle with remaining dressing. Serve with wontons.

prep & cook *30 minutes*   serves *4*
nutritional count per serving *18.1g total fat (3.1g
saturated fat); 1208kJ (289 cal); 4g carbohydrate;
27g protein; 1.2g fibre*

salt & pepper squid salad

garlic prawns & tat soi salad

barbecued pork & noodle salad

tandoori chicken & spinach salad

barbecued pork & noodle salad

10 trimmed red radishes (150g), sliced thinly,
    cut into matchsticks
1 large red capsicum (350g) sliced thinly
2 baby buk choy (300g), sliced thinly
6 green onions, sliced thinly
1 cup (80g) bean sprouts
½ cup (70g) roasted slivered almonds
2 x 100g packets fried noodles
400g chinese barbecued pork, sliced thinly

sweet-sour dressing
¼ cup (60ml) peanut oil
2 tablespoons white vinegar
2 tablespoons brown sugar
2 tablespoons light soy sauce
1 teaspoon sesame oil
1 clove garlic, crushed

1 Place ingredients for sweet-sour dressing in screw-top jar; shake well.

2 Place salad ingredients in large bowl with dressing; toss gently to combine.

prep time *20 minutes* serves *6*
nutritional count per serving *29.7g total fat (7.6g saturated fat); 1789kJ (428 cal); 17.6g carbohydrate; 20.4g protein; 6.1g fibre*

tandoori chicken & spinach salad

⅓ cup (100g) tandoori paste
¼ cup (70g) yogurt
800g chicken tenderloins
1 tablespoon vegetable oil
8 large uncooked pappadums
150g baby spinach leaves, trimmed
2 lebanese cucumbers (260g), sliced thickly
250g cherry tomatoes, halved
1 cup firmly packed fresh mint leaves

spiced yogurt
1 clove garlic, crushed
¾ cup (210g) yogurt
1 tablespoon lemon juice
1 teaspoon ground cumin
1 teaspoon ground coriander

1 Combine paste and yogurt in medium bowl with chicken. Cover; refrigerate 3 hours or overnight.

2 Combine ingredients for spiced yogurt in small jug.

3 Heat oil in large frying pan; cook chicken mixture, in batches, until cooked through.

4 Microwave 2 pappadums at a time on HIGH (100%) about 30 seconds.

5 Place chicken in large bowl with spinach, cucumber, tomato and mint; toss gently to combine. Drizzle with yogurt; serve with pappadums.

prep & cook time *35 minutes (+ refrigeration)* serves *4*
nutritional count per serving *12.5g total fat (3.4g saturated fat); 1731kJ (414 cal); 16.4g carbohydrate; 55.1g protein; 6.7g fibre*

salmon & pickled ginger salad

100g rice vermicelli noodles
800g salmon fillets, skin on
3 shallots (75g), sliced thinly
1 cup loosely packed fresh coriander leaves
2 tablespoons drained pickled ginger in syrup,
    sliced finely

sesame soy dressing
1 tablespoon toasted sesame seeds
2 tablespoons lemon juice
1 tablespoon pickled ginger syrup (see note below)
1 tablespoon light soy sauce
1 tablespoon kecap manis
2 teaspoons sesame oil
2 teaspoons olive oil

1 Place noodles in large heatproof bowl; cover with boiling water. Stand until just tender; drain. Rinse under cold water; drain.

2 Meanwhile, cook fish, skin-side down, on heated oiled grill plate (or grill or barbecue) about 5 minutes or until skin is crisp. Turn fish; cook about 4 minutes or until cooked as desired. Lift skin from fish; cook skin, on same grill plate, until crisp. Slice skin finely; flake fish into large pieces.

3 Combine ingredients for sesame soy dressing in small bowl.

4 Place noodles in large bowl with shallot, coriander, ginger and half the dressing; toss gently to combine, then divide among serving plates. Top with fish, drizzle with remaining dressing; sprinkle with crisp salmon skin.

prep & cook time *35 minutes* serves *4*
nutritional count per serving *20.7g total fat (4g saturated fat); 1793kJ (429 cal); 17.7g carbohydrate; 42.3g protein; 1.3g fibre*

For the pickled ginger syrup in the dressing, use the syrup drained from the pickled ginger in the salad.

lime & coconut snake bean salad

350g snake beans, chopped coarsely
½ cup (50g) coarsely grated fresh coconut
¾ cup loosely packed fresh coriander leaves

lime and coconut dressing
¼ cup (60ml) coconut cream
1 tablespoon lime juice
2 teaspoons fish sauce
1 long green chilli, chopped finely

1   Boil, steam or microwave beans until tender; drain.

2   Meanwhile, place ingredients for lime and coconut dressing in screw-top jar; shake well.

3   Place beans in medium bowl with remaining ingredients and dressing; toss gently to combine.

prep & cook time *20 minutes*   serves *4*
nutritional count per serving   *11.5g total fat (9.9g saturated fat); 598kJ (143 cal); 3.2g carbohydrate; 4.5g protein; 4.9g fibre*

To open fresh coconut, pierce one of the eyes then roast coconut briefly in a very hot oven only until cracks appear in the shell. Cool the coconut, then break it apart and grate the flesh.

tuna & soba noodle salad

270g soba noodles
700g tuna steaks
1 lebanese cucumber (130g), seeded, sliced thinly
2 green onions, sliced thinly
1 sheet nori, shredded finely
1 tablespoon black cumin seeds

coriander dressing
½ cup firmly packed fresh coriander leaves
¼ cup (60ml) light olive oil
¼ cup (60ml) lemon juice
2 tablespoons rice wine vinegar
1 teaspoon sesame oil
1cm piece fresh ginger (5g), grated
1 clove garlic, quartered

1   Cook noodles in large saucepan of boiling water until tender; drain. Rinse under cold water; drain.

2   Meanwhile, make coriander dressing.

3   Cook fish on heated oiled grill plate (or grill or barbecue) until cooked as desired. Slice fish thickly.

4   Place noodles in large bowl with cucumber, onion, nori, seeds and dressing; toss gently to combine. Divide salad among serving plates; top with fish.

coriander dressing   Blend or process ingredients until combined.

prep & cook time *30 minutes*   serves *6*
nutritional count per serving   *17.1g total fat (4.2g saturated fat); 1781kJ (426 cal); 31.8g carbohydrate; 34.8g protein; 2.3g fibre*

lime & coconut snake bean salad

tuna & soba noodle salad

asian millet & tofu salad

asian-style coleslaw

asian millet & tofu salad

1 cup (200g) millet
2 fresh long red chillies, chopped finely
⅓ cup (45g) roasted unsalted coarsely
    chopped peanuts
400g firm marinated tofu, cut into batons
100g snow peas, trimmed, sliced lengthways
230g can bamboo shoots, rinsed, drained, sliced thinly
½ small red onion (50g), sliced thinly

japanese dressing
¼ cup (60ml) mirin
1 tablespoon japanese soy sauce
1 tablespoon rice vinegar
1 clove garlic, crushed

1 Cook millet in medium saucepan of boiling water, uncovered, until just tender; drain. Cool.

2 Meanwhile, place ingredients for japanese dressing in screw-top jar; shake well.

3 Place millet in large bowl with chilli, nuts and half the dressing; stir to combine.

4 Place tofu in medium bowl with remaining ingredients and dressing; toss gently to combine.

5 Serve millet mixture topped with tofu salad.

prep & cook time *35 minutes* serves *4*
nutritional count per serving *14.4g total fat (2.2g saturated fat); 1676kJ (401 cal); 39.3g carbohydrate; 22g protein; 8.8g fibre*

asian-style coleslaw

2 cups (160g) finely shredded wombok
1 medium carrot (120g), grated coarsely
3 green onions, sliced thinly
1 cup loosely packed fresh coriander leaves
100g crispy fried noodles

plum and soy dressing
2 tablespoons peanut oil
1 tablespoon plum sauce
1 tablespoon white wine vinegar
2 teaspoons light soy sauce
1 teaspoon caster sugar

1 Place ingredients for plum and soy dressing in screw-top jar; shake well.

2 Place salad ingredients in large bowl with dressing; toss gently to combine.

prep time *15 minutes* serves *4*
nutritional count per serving *5.6g total fat (1.1g saturated fat); 602kJ (144 cal); 18.7g carbohydrate; 3.5g protein; 2.3g fibre*

pork sang choy bow

1 teaspoon sesame oil
1 small yellow capsicum (150g), sliced thinly
1 small brown onion (80g), sliced thinly
2 cloves garlic, crushed
2cm piece fresh ginger (10g), grated
250g pork fillet, minced
2 tablespoons light soy sauce
2 tablespoons oyster sauce
1 tablespoon lime juice
3 cups (240g) bean sprouts
4 green onions, sliced thinly
¼ cup coarsely chopped fresh coriander
8 large butter lettuce leaves

1 Heat oil in wok; stir-fry capsicum, brown onion, garlic and ginger until onion softens. Add pork; stir-fry until changed in colour.

2 Add sauces and juice; stir-fry until combined. Remove from heat; toss sprouts, green onion and coriander into pork mixture.

3 Spoon sang choy bow mixture into lettuce leaves to serve.

prep & cook time *30 minutes* serves *4*
nutritional count per serving *2.9g total fat (0.7g saturated fat); 568kJ (136 cal); 7.2g carbohydrate; 18.1g protein; 3.6g fibre*

prawn & soba noodle salad

270g dried soba noodles
20 uncooked medium king prawns (900g)
1 medium carrot (120g), cut into matchsticks
1 small daikon (400g), cut into matchsticks
2 green onions, sliced thinly
1 fresh long red chilli, sliced thinly
½ sheet toasted nori (yaki-nori), shredded finely

soy dressing
2 tablespoons rice vinegar
2 tablespoons water
1 tablespoon japanese soy sauce
½ teaspoon white sugar

1 Cook noodles in medium saucepan of boiling water, uncovered, until just tender; drain. Rinse noodles under cold water; drain.

2 Meanwhile, place ingredients for soy dressing in screw-top jar; shake well.

3 Shell and devein prawns; cut in half lengthways. Cook prawns in medium saucepan of boiling water, uncovered, until changed in colour. Drain; cool.

4 Combine noodles, prawns and dressing in large bowl with carrot, daikon, onion and chilli. Serve salad sprinkled with nori.

prep & cook time *20 minutes*   serves *6*
nutritional count per serving *1.1g total fat (0.2g saturated fat); 1003kJ (240 cal); 33.8g carbohydrate; 21.3g protein; 3.1g fibre*

rump steak & sprout salad

1 tablespoon black bean sauce
1 tablespoon honey
1 fresh long red chilli, chopped finely
3cm piece fresh ginger (15g), grated
600g piece beef rump steak
¼ cup (60ml) lime juice
1 tablespoon peanut oil
2 teaspoons honey, extra
100g snow pea sprouts, trimmed
1 large red capsicum (350g), sliced thinly
1 lebanese cucumber (130g), seeded, sliced thinly

1 Combine sauce, honey, chilli and a third of the ginger in large bowl with beef, coat all over with mixture.

2 Cook beef on heated oiled grill plate (or grill or barbecue) until browned both sides and cooked as desired. Cover beef, stand 5 minutes then slice thickly.

3 Meanwhile, whisk remaining ginger with juice, oil and extra honey in large bowl. Add sprouts, capsicum, cucumber and dressing; toss gently to combine. Serve salad with beef.

prep & cook time *25 minutes* serves *4*
nutritional count per serving *15.2g total fat (5.4g saturated fat); 1547kJ (370 cal); 19.3g carbohydrate; 37.6g protein; 2.6g fibre.*

pork belly & nashi salad

1kg boneless pork belly, rind on
2 teaspoons sea salt flakes
750g choy sum, trimmed, sliced thinly
2 medium nashi (400g), cut into matchsticks
2 green onions, sliced thinly
1 fresh long red chilli, cut into matchsticks

plum and five-spice dressing
¼ cup (60ml) vegetable oil
2 tablespoons rice vinegar
1 tablespoon plum sauce
½ teaspoon five-spice powder

1 Score pork rind at 1cm intervals; rub salt all over pork rind. Place pork, rind-side up, on wire rack over large baking dish. Cover loosely; refrigerate overnight.

2 Preheat oven to 220°C/200°C fan-forced.

3 Roast pork, uncovered, 45 minutes. Reduce oven temperature to 180°C/160°C fan-forced. Roast pork, uncovered, a further 30 minutes or until rind is crisp and pork is cooked as desired. Stand pork, uncovered, 5 minutes then slice thinly.

4 Meanwhile, combine ingredients for plum and five-spice dressing in screw-top jar; shake well.

5 Combine choy sum, nashi, onion and chilli in large bowl with half the dressing.

6 Divide salad among serving plates; top with pork, drizzle with remaining dressing.

prep & cook time *1 hour 30 minutes (+ refrigeration)* serves *6*
nutritional count per serving *46.7g total fat (13.8g saturated fat); 2462kJ (589 cal); 9.8g carbohydrate; 31.8g protein; 2.9g fibre*

Rubbing salt on the pork and leaving it overnight draws moisture out of the rind, drying it out – this helps to make perfect crackling. Ask your butcher to score the rind as they have the best tools for the job.

rump steak & sprout salad

pork belly & nashi salad

soba & daikon salad

green mango salad with tuna

soba & daikon salad

300g dried soba noodles
1 small daikon (400g), cut into matchsticks
4 green onions, sliced thinly
1 teaspoon sesame oil
100g enoki mushrooms
2 tablespoons thinly sliced pickled ginger
1 toasted seaweed sheet (yaki-nori), sliced thinly

mirin dressing
¼ cup (60ml) mirin
2 tablespoons kecap manis
1 tablespoon sake
1 clove garlic, crushed
1cm piece fresh ginger (5g), grated
1 teaspoon white sugar

1 Cook noodles in large saucepan of boiling water, uncovered, until just tender; drain. Rinse under cold water; drain.

2 Place ingredients for mirin dressing in screw-top jar; shake well.

3 Place noodles in large bowl with daikon, onion and half of the dressing; toss gently to combine.

4 Heat oil in small frying pan; cook mushrooms, stirring, 2 minutes.

5 Divide soba salad among serving plates; top with combined mushrooms, ginger and seaweed. Drizzle with remaining dressing.

prep & cook time *35 minutes* serves *4*
nutritional count per serving *2.4g total fat (0.3g saturated fat); 1292kJ (309 cal); 56.6g carbohydrate; 10.9g protein; 5.3g fibre*

green mango salad with tuna

1 green mango (350g)
2 teaspoons sesame oil
800g tuna steaks, cut into 3cm pieces
½ teaspoon dried chilli flakes
2 tablespoons toasted sesame seeds
2 cups (100g) snow pea sprouts
½ cup firmly packed fresh coriander leaves
½ cup firmly packed fresh mint leaves
½ small red onion (50g), sliced thinly

lime and ginger dressing
¼ cup (60ml) lime juice
3cm piece fresh ginger (15g), grated
1 tablespoon fish sauce

1 Place ingredients for lime and ginger dressing in screw-top jar; shake well.

2 Using vegetable peeler, slice mango into thin ribbons.

3 Combine oil and fish in medium bowl. Cook fish on heated oiled grill plate (or grill or barbecue).

4 Return fish to same cleaned bowl with chilli and seeds; mix gently.

5 Place snow pea sprouts in medium bowl with remaining ingredients and dressing; toss gently to combine. Serve salad topped with fish.

prep & cook time *40 minutes* serves *4*
nutritional count per serving *17.8g total fat (5.4g saturated fat); 1894kJ (453 cal); 15.5g carbohydrate; 55.5g protein; 3.7g fibre*

vietnamese chicken salad

500g chicken breast fillets
1 large carrot (180g)
½ cup (125ml) rice wine vinegar
2 teaspoons salt
2 tablespoons caster sugar
1 medium white onion (150g), sliced thinly
1½ cups (120g) bean sprouts
2 cups (160g) finely shredded savoy cabbage
¼ cup firmly packed fresh vietnamese mint leaves
½ cup firmly packed fresh coriander leaves
1 tablespoon crushed roasted peanuts
2 tablespoons fried shallots

vietnamese dressing
2 tablespoons fish sauce
¼ cup (60ml) water
2 tablespoons caster sugar
2 tablespoons lime juice
1 clove garlic, crushed

1 Place chicken in medium saucepan of boiling water; return to the boil. Reduce heat; simmer, uncovered, about 10 minutes or until cooked through. Cool chicken in poaching liquid 10 minutes; discard liquid (or reserve for another use). Shred chicken coarsely.

2 Meanwhile, cut carrot into matchstick-sized pieces. Combine carrot, vinegar, salt and sugar in large bowl, cover; stand 5 minutes. Add onion, cover; stand 5 minutes. Add sprouts, cover; stand 3 minutes. Drain pickled vegetables; discard liquid.

3 Place ingredients for vietnamese dressing in screw-top jar; shake well.

4 Place pickled vegetables in large bowl with chicken, cabbage, mint, coriander and dressing; toss gently to combine. Sprinkle with nuts and shallots.

prep & cook time *35 minutes*   serves *4*
nutritional count per serving *8.9g total fat (2.3g saturated fat); 1271kJ (304 cal); 24.3g carbohydrate; 31g protein; 5.1g fibre*

coconut chicken & noodle salad

600g chicken breast fillets
1 cup (250ml) light coconut cream
1½ cups (375ml) chicken stock
1 tablespoon brown sugar
1 clove garlic, crushed
2cm piece fresh ginger (10g), grated
1 tablespoon fish sauce
2 tablespoons lime juice
125g rice vermicelli noodles
1 small carrot (70g), sliced thinly
¼ cup (50g) drained sliced bamboo shoots, rinsed
¼ cup loosely packed fresh coriander leaves,
    chopped finely
¼ cup loosely packed fresh mint leaves,
    chopped finely

1   Place chicken in medium saucepan with cream, stock, sugar, garlic and ginger; bring to the boil. Reduce heat; simmer, uncovered, about 10 minutes or until cooked. Cool chicken in poaching liquid 10 minutes. Remove chicken from pan. Return poaching liquid to the boil; reduce to 1 cup. Remove from heat; stir in sauce and juice.

2   Meanwhile, place noodles in large heatproof bowl, cover with boiling water; stand until just tender, drain. Rinse under cold water; drain. Using scissors, cut noodles into random lengths.

3   Tear chicken coarsely. Place noodles and chicken in medium bowl with carrot and bamboo shoots; stir in poaching liquid. Serve sprinkled with herbs.

prep & cook time *50 minutes*   serves *4*
nutritional count per serving   *11.5g total fat (7.9g saturated fat); 1346kJ (322 cal); 16.1g carbohydrate; 37.6g protein; 1.5g fibre*

green papaya & pork salad

½ cup (125ml) water
600g pork fillets
1 small green papaya (650g)
1 large carrot (180g)
2 teaspoons vegetable oil
1 cup firmly packed fresh coriander leaves
⅓ cup (45g) coarsely chopped roasted unsalted peanuts

chilli and tamarind dressing
4 cloves garlic, crushed
4 fresh small red thai chillies, chopped finely
⅔ cup (200g) tamarind concentrate
1 tablespoon finely grated lime rind
½ cup (125ml) lime juice
2 shallots (50g), sliced thinly
⅓ cup grated palm sugar

1   Combine ingredients for chilli and tamarind dressing in small jug.

2   Place the water in large frying pan with ½ cup of the dressing. Add pork; bring to the boil. Reduce heat; simmer, covered, 20 minutes or until pork is cooked through. Remove pork from pan; cover, stand pork 10 minutes then slice thinly.

3   Peel then halve papaya; remove seeds. Using vegetable peeler, slice papaya and carrot lengthways into thin strips.

4   Stir oil into remaining dressing. Place pork and papaya in medium bowl with carrot, coriander and dressing; toss gently to combine. Serve salad topped with nuts.

prep & cook time *45 minutes*   serves *4*
nutritional count per serving   *11.4g total fat (2.3g saturated fat); 1643kJ (393 cal); 31.7g carbohydrate; 37.9g protein; 6.6g fibre*

coconut chicken & noodle salad

green papaya & pork salad

asian crispy noodle salad

thai herb & mango salad

asian crispy noodle salad

½ medium wombok (500g), shredded finely
227g can water chestnuts, drained, sliced thinly
150g snow peas, trimmed, sliced thinly
1 large red capsicum (350g), sliced thinly
100g packet fried noodles
½ cup (50g) roasted unsalted cashews,
    chopped coarsely
1 cup loosely packed fresh coriander leaves

sesame soy dressing
1 teaspoon sesame oil
¼ cup (60ml) soy sauce
1 tablespoon sweet chilli sauce
2 tablespoons lime juice

1 Place ingredients for sesame soy dressing in screw-top jar; shake well.

2 Place wombok, water chestnuts, snow peas, capsicum and fried noodles in medium bowl; toss gently to combine.

3 Divide salad among serving bowls; sprinkle with nuts and coriander, drizzle with dressing.

prep time *15 minutes* serves *4*
nutritional count per serving *10.8g fat (2.2g saturated fat); 869kJ (208 cal); 19.1g carbohydrate; 8.3g protein; 6.4g fibre*

thai herb & mango salad

2 medium mangoes (860g)
10cm stick fresh lemon grass (20g), sliced thinly
2 fresh long red chillies, cut into thin strips
150g snow peas, trimmed, sliced thinly
6 green onions, sliced thinly
1 cup (80g) bean sprouts
½ cup loosely packed fresh coriander leaves
¼ cup loosely packed fresh mint leaves
¼ cup loosely packed vietnamese mint leaves
1 tablespoon coarsely shredded thai basil

palm sugar and lime dressing
¼ cup (60ml) lime juice
1 tablespoon fish sauce
2 tablespoons grated palm sugar
2 cloves garlic, crushed

1 Place ingredients for palm sugar and lime dressing in screw-top jar; shake well.

2 Slice cheeks from mangoes; cut each cheek into thin strips.

3 Place mango in large bowl with remaining ingredients and dressing; toss gently to combine.

prep time *25 minutes* serves *4*
nutritional count per serving *0.6g total fat (0g saturated fat); 631kJ (151 cal); 29.3g carbohydrate; 4.5g protein; 5g fibre*

middle-eastern salads

grilled lamb & chickpea salad, page 176

Middle-eastern salads are made from couscous, chickpeas, burghul and wonderful spices. Lamb is a favourite meat and haloumi is a favourite cheese, fried in olive oil and served warm.

grilled lamb & chickpea salad

3 cloves garlic, crushed
¼ cup (60ml) lemon juice
1 tablespoon olive oil
2 teaspoons ground cumin
750g lamb backstraps
2 tablespoons lemon juice, extra
2 tablespoons olive oil, extra
800g can chickpeas, rinsed, drained
3 medium egg tomatoes (225g), cut into wedges
1 lebanese cucumber (130g), halved lengthways, sliced on the diagonal
1 medium red onion (170g), sliced thinly
½ cup coarsely chopped fresh mint
½ cup coarsely chopped fresh flat-leaf parsley

1 Combine garlic, juice, oil and cumin in large bowl with lamb. Refrigerate 3 hours or overnight.

2 Drain lamb; reserve marinade. Cook lamb on heated, oiled grill plate (or grill or barbecue), brushing occasionally with marinade. Cover; stand 5 minutes then slice thinly.

3 Whisk extra juice and extra oil in large bowl, add remaining ingredients; toss gently to combine. Serve salad topped with lamb.

prep & cook time *35 minutes (+ refrigeration)* serves *4*
nutritional count per serving *33.2g total fat (9.8g saturated fat); 2537kJ (607 cal); 23.3g carbohydrate; 49.5g protein; 9.1g fibre*

burghul salad with chickpeas

1 large red capsicum (350g)
1 cup (160g) burghul
1 cup (250ml) boiling water
420g can chickpeas, rinsed, drained
1 stalk celery (150g), trimmed, chopped finely
50g baby spinach leaves

sumac and herb dressing
1 tablespoon sesame seeds
2 tablespoons sumac
1 tablespoon fresh thyme leaves
1 tablespoon coarsely chopped fresh oregano
½ cup (125ml) lime juice
1 tablespoon olive oil
1 clove garlic, crushed

1 Quarter capsicum; discard seeds and membranes. Roast under grill or in very hot oven, skin-side up, until skin blisters and blackens. Cover capsicum pieces with plastic or paper for 5 minutes; peel away skin, then slice capsicum thinly.

2 Meanwhile, place burghul in medium bowl, cover with the boiling water; stand about 10 minutes or until burghul softens and water is absorbed.

3 Combine ingredients for sumac and herb dressing in small bowl.

4 Place burghul and capsicum in large bowl with chickpeas, celery, spinach and dressing; toss gently to combine.

prep & cook time *30 minutes* serves *4*
nutritional count per serving *8.6g total fat (1.2g saturated fat); 1150kJ (275 cal); 37.3g carbohydrate; 11.2g protein; 11.8g fibre*

burghul salad with chickpeas

couscous salad with chickpeas

haloumi & pomegranate salad

couscous salad with chickpeas

1½ cups (300g) couscous
1½ cups (375ml) boiling water
20g butter
420g can chickpeas, rinsed, drained
⅓ cup (55g) sultanas
⅓ cup (50g) roasted pine nuts
100g baby rocket leaves, chopped coarsely
¾ cup finely chopped fresh flat-leaf parsley
1 cup (120g) seeded green olives

preserved lemon dressing
1 tablespoon finely grated lemon rind
¼ cup (60ml) lemon juice
¼ cup (60ml) olive oil
2 tablespoons rinsed and drained finely chopped
    preserved lemon

1 Combine couscous with the water in large heatproof
bowl, cover; stand about 5 minutes or until water is
absorbed, fluffing with fork occasionally. Stir in butter.
Stand 10 minutes.

2 Place ingredients for preserved lemon dressing in
screw-top jar; shake well.

3 Place couscous in large bowl with remaining
ingredients and dressing; toss gently to combine.

prep time *20 minutes* serves *4*
nutritional count per serving *29g total fat (5.5g
saturated fat); 268kJ (686 cal); 85.6g carbohydrate;
17.2g protein; 6.5g fibre*

haloumi & pomegranate salad

1 tablespoon lemon juice
2 tablespoons light olive oil
⅓ cup (80ml) pomegranate pulp
¼ cup firmly packed fresh mint leaves
2 green onions, sliced thinly
125g mizuna
1 medium fennel (300g), trimmed, sliced thinly
360g haloumi cheese, sliced thickly

1 Combine juice, oil, pulp, mint, onion, mizuna and fennel
in large bowl.

2 Brown cheese, both sides, in large oiled frying pan.
Serve salad topped with cheese.

prep & cook time *20 minutes* serves *4*
nutritional count per serving *24.7g total fat (11.2g
saturated fat); 1400kJ (335 cal); 6.5g carbohydrate;
20.6g protein; 3.5g fibre*

za'atar lamb with warm chickpea salad

1 cup (200g) dried chickpeas
1 bay leaf
800g lamb backstraps
¼ cup (60ml) olive oil
1 tablespoon sumac
1 tablespoon toasted sesame seeds
1 teaspoon dried thyme leaves
1 teaspoon dried oregano leaves
1 teaspoon dried marjoram leaves
1 teaspoon sweet paprika
20g butter
12 baby onions (300g), halved
1 large carrot (180g), chopped finely
2 trimmed celery stalks (200g), chopped finely
2 small fennel bulbs (400g), trimmed, sliced thinly
1 cup firmly packed fresh flat-leaf parsley

sumac dressing
1 tablespoon sumac
1 teaspoon dijon mustard
¼ cup (60ml) olive oil
¼ cup (60ml) lemon juice

1 Place chickpeas in large bowl of cold water; stand overnight. Drain.

2 Cook chickpeas and bay leaf in medium saucepan of boiling water, uncovered, until just tender; drain. Rinse under cold water; drain.

3 Meanwhile, place lamb, 2 tablespoons of the oil and combined sumac, seeds, dried herbs and paprika in large bowl; toss to coat lamb. Cover; refrigerate 30 minutes.

4 Place ingredients for sumac dressing in screw-top jar; shake well.

5 Heat butter and remaining oil in large frying pan; cook onion, stirring, about 10 minutes or until browned lightly and softened. Add carrot, celery and fennel; cook, stirring, until vegetables are just tender.

6 Meanwhile, cook lamb, in batches, on heated oiled grill plate (or grill or barbecue) until browned and cooked as desired. Cover; stand 5 minutes. Slice lamb thickly.

7 Just before serving, combine chickpeas, parsley and half of the dressing with vegetables; cook, stirring, until heated through. Divide chickpea salad among serving plates; top with lamb, drizzle with remaining dressing.

prep & cook time *1 hour 25 minutes (+ standing and refrigeration)* serves *4*
nutritional count per serving *52.3g total fat (15g saturated fat); 3119kJ (746 cal); 17.1g carbohydrate; 48.9g protein; 8.4g fibre*

roasted pumpkin, carrot & parsnip salad

900g piece pumpkin, unpeeled, sliced thinly
1 tablespoon olive oil
4 large carrots (720g), halved, sliced thickly
2 large parsnips (700g), chopped coarsely
⅓ cup firmly packed fresh flat-leaf parsley leaves
¼ cup (40g) roasted pine nuts

spice paste
2 cloves garlic, quartered
1 teaspoon cumin seeds
1 teaspoon coriander seeds
½ teaspoon ground cinnamon
1 teaspoon sea salt
1 tablespoon olive oil
20g butter
¼ cup (55g) firmly packed brown sugar
1½ cups (375ml) apple juice

1 Preheat oven to 200°C/180°C fan-forced.

2 Place pumpkin and oil in large baking dish; toss pumpkin to coat in oil. Roast, uncovered, about 25 minutes or until just tender.

3 Meanwhile, boil, steam or microwave carrot and parsnip, separately, until just tender; drain. Make spice paste.

4 Place vegetables, parsley and nuts in large bowl with spice mixture; toss gently to combine.

spice paste Using mortar and pestle or small electric spice blender, crush garlic, cumin, coriander, cinnamon, salt and oil until mixture forms a thick paste. Melt butter in large frying pan; cook paste, stirring, about 3 minutes or until fragrant. Add sugar and juice; bring to the boil. Cook, stirring, about 10 minutes or until spice mixture thickens slightly.

prep & cook time *40 minutes* serves *8*
nutritional count per serving *10.7g total fat (2.5g saturated fat); 1032kJ (247 cal); 29.9g carbohydrate; 4.8g protein; 5.8g fibre*

grilled lamb with burghul salad

¾ cup (120g) burghul
1 tablespoon olive oil
1 tablespoon ras el hanout
800g lamb backstraps
½ cup (70g) roasted unsalted pistachios,
    chopped coarsely
1 small red onion (100g), chopped finely
¾ cup loosely packed fresh parsley leaves
¾ cup loosely packed fresh mint leaves
⅓ cup (55g) dried currants
1 tablespoons finely grated lemon rind
1 clove garlic, crushed
¼ cup (60ml) lemon juice
2 tablespoons olive oil, extra

1 Place burghul in medium bowl, cover with water.
Stand 10 minutes; drain. Squeeze out as much excess
water as possible.

2 Combine oil, spice and lamb in medium bowl,
turn to coat lamb in mixture. Cook lamb, in batches,
on heated oiled grill plate (or grill or barbecue) until
browned both sides and cooked as desired. Cover lamb;
stand 10 minutes, then slice thickly.

3 Add remaining ingredients to burghul; toss gently
to combine. Serve salad topped with sliced lamb and,
if you like, a dollop of yogurt.

prep & cook time *40 minutes* serves *4*
nutritional count per serving *30.7g total fat (6.3g
saturated fat); 2776kJ (664 cal); 38.5g carbohydrate;
53g protein; 10.8g fibre*

chermoulla chicken salad

1 cup (200g) dried chickpeas
4 single chicken breast fillets (680g)
1 medium red capsicum (150g), chopped finely
1 medium green capsicum (150g), chopped finely
2 large egg tomatoes (180g), chopped finely
1 small white onion (80g), chopped finely
2 tablespoons lemon juice

chermoulla
½ cup finely chopped fresh coriander
½ cup finely chopped fresh flat-leaf parsley
3 cloves garlic, crushed
2 tablespoons white wine vinegar
2 tablespoons lemon juice
1 teaspoon sweet paprika
½ teaspoon ground cumin
2 tablespoons olive oil

1 Place chickpeas in large bowl of cold water; stand
overnight, drain. Rinse under cold water; drain. Cook
chickpeas in medium saucepan of boiling water, uncovered,
until just tender; drain. Rinse under cold water; drain.

2 Meanwhile, combine ingredients for chermoulla in large
bowl; reserve half of the chermoulla for chickpea salad.

3 Place chicken in bowl with remaining half of the chermoulla;
turn chicken to coat in chermoulla. Cook chicken, in batches,
on heated oiled grill plate (or grill or barbecue) until cooked
through. Cover to keep warm.

4 Place chickpeas in large bowl with capsicums, tomato,
onion and remaining chermoulla; toss gently to combine.
Serve salad with sliced chicken, drizzled with juice.

prep & cook time *40 minutes (+ standing)* serves *4*
nutritional count per serving *21.6g total fat (4.6g
saturated fat); 1994kJ (477 cal); 22.5g carbohydrate;
47.2g protein; 9g fibre*

grilled lamb with burghul salad

chermoulla chicken salad

tomato & herb salad with toasted lavash

¼ cup (40g) burghul
2 tablespoons lemon juice
1 piece lavash bread (60g), cut into wedges
2 cups loosely packed fresh flat-leaf parsley leaves
1 cup coarsely chopped fresh mint
2 green onions, sliced thinly
¼ cup (60ml) olive oil
4 medium tomatoes (450g), cut into 1cm thick slices

1 Combine burghul and juice in small bowl. Cover; refrigerate 1 hour.

2 Meanwhile, preheat oven to 180°C/160°C fan-forced.

3 Place bread on oven tray; bake 5 minutes or until crisp.

4 Place burghul mixture in medium bowl with parsley, mint, onion and oil; stir to combine.

5 Stack tomato slices with burghul mixture on serving plates; accompany with bread pieces. Drizzle extra olive oil around stack, if you like.

prep & cook time *15 minutes (+ refrigeration)* serves 4
nutritional count per serving *14.5g total fat (2g saturated fat); 957kJ (229 cal); 17.4g carbohydrate; 4.7g protein; 5.9g fibre*

sumac, onion & mint salad

4 small red onions (400g), sliced thinly
2 tablespoons olive oil
2 tablespoons finely chopped fresh mint
1 tablespoon lemon juice
1 tablespoon sumac

1 Place ingredients in medium bowl; toss gently to combine.

prep time *10 minutes* serves *8*
nutritional count per serving *4.6g total fat (0.6g saturated fat); 238kJ (57 cal); 2.8g carbohydrate; 0.7g protein; 0.7g fibre*

mixed vegetable salad with baba ghanoush

1 large green capsicum (350g)
1 large red capsicum (350g)
1 large yellow capsicum (350g)
1 large eggplant (500g)
2 cloves garlic, unpeeled
1 tablespoon lemon juice
1 tablespoon tahini
½ cup (125ml) olive oil
350g cap mushrooms, sliced thickly
1 sprig fresh thyme
250g cherry tomatoes
20 baby zucchini (200g), halved
8 yellow patty-pan squash (250g), halved
2 small fennel bulbs (400g) trimmed, quartered
12 shallots (300g), peeled
⅓ cup (80ml) dry white wine
1 long loaf turkish bread
½ cup loosely packed fresh flat-leaf parsley leaves

1 Preheat oven to 240°C/220°C fan-forced.

2 Quarter capsicums, discard seeds and membranes. Using fork, prick eggplant all over; place on oiled oven tray with garlic and capsicum, skin-side up. Roast vegetables, uncovered, about 30 minutes or until skins blister. Cover capsicum pieces with plastic or paper for 5 minutes; peel away skin then slice thickly.

3 When cool enough to handle, peel eggplant and garlic. Blend or process eggplant, garlic, juice and tahini until mixture forms a paste. With motor operating, pour in half of the oil in a thin, steady stream until eggplant mixture is pureed. Reserve.

4 Meanwhile, toss mushrooms and thyme with 1 tablespoon of the remaining oil in large shallow baking dish. Toss tomatoes, zucchini, squash and 1 tablespoon of the remaining oil in another large shallow baking dish. Roast, uncovered, about 20 minutes or until mushrooms and vegetables are just tender.

5 Heat remaining oil in medium saucepan; cook fennel and shallots, stirring occasionally, about 5 minutes or until vegetables are browned lightly. Add wine; cook, covered, about 20 minutes or until vegetables are tender, stirring occasionally. Drain vegetables; add cooking liquid to processor with eggplant puree, process until smooth. This mixture is the baba ghanoush.

6 Quarter bread; slice quarters horizontally. Place on oiled grill plate (or grill or barbecue) until browned lightly both sides. Divide bread among serving plates; top with combined mushrooms, vegetables and parsley. Serve with baba ghanoush.

prep & cook time *1 hour 50 minutes* serves *4*
nutritional count per serving *39.9g total fat (4.7g saturated fat); 2558kJ (612 cal); 45.7g carbohydrate; 18.5g protein; 15.7g fibre*

couscous tabbouleh

fattoush with harissa lamb

middle-eastern salads

couscous tabbouleh

2 cups (400g) couscous
2 cups (500ml) boiling water
2 teaspoons finely grated lemon rind
4 medium egg tomatoes (300g), seeded,
   chopped finely
1 lebanese cucumber (130g), seeded, chopped finely
1 small red onion (100g), chopped finely
1 cup coarsely chopped fresh flat-leaf parsley
400g can chickpeas, rinsed, drained

lemon mint dressing
½ cup (140g) low-fat natural yogurt
2 tablespoons lemon juice
2 teaspoons finely chopped fresh mint

1   Combine couscous with the water and lemon rind
in large heatproof bowl, cover; stand 5 minutes or until
liquid is absorbed, fluffing with fork occasionally.

2   Meanwhile, combine ingredients for lemon mint
dressing in small bowl.

3   Add tomato, cucumber, onion, parsley and chickpeas
to couscous; toss gently to combine. Serve salad drizzled
with dressing.

prep & cook time *15 minutes* serves *4*
nutritional count per serving *2.2g total fat (0.3g
saturated fat); 2011kJ (481 cal); 90.6g carbohydrate;
20.3g protein; 5.8g fibre*

fattoush with harissa lamb

600g lamb backstraps
¼ cup (75g) harissa
3 pocket pittas (255g)
¼ cup (60ml) olive oil
3 medium tomatoes (450g), cut into wedges
1 large green capsicum (350g), sliced thickly
2 lebanese cucumbers (260g), halved, sliced thinly
½ cup coarsely chopped fresh mint
1 cup firmly packed fresh flat-leaf parsley leaves
¼ cup (60ml) lemon juice
1 clove garlic, crushed

1   Combine lamb and harissa in medium bowl; rub harissa
into lamb. Refrigerate 1 hour.

2   Preheat grill.

3   Heat 1 tablespoon of the oil in large frying pan; cook lamb.
Cover; stand 5 minutes, then slice thickly.

4   Split pittas in half; grill both sides until browned lightly.

5   To make fattoush, place remaining ingredients in large bowl;
toss gently to combine. Break pitta into pieces over fattoush.
Serve fattoush topped with lamb.

prep & cook time *45 minutes (+ refrigeration)* serves *4*
nutritional count per serving *28.9g total fat (8.2g
saturated fat); 2416kJ (578 cal); 36.7g carbohydrate;
39.6g protein; 6.4g fibre*

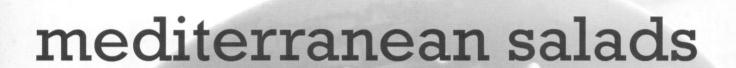

mediterranean salads

193

panzanella with radish sandwiches, page 196

Tomatoes, olives, olive oil, zucchini,
eggplant, garlic – all those wonderful
Mediterranean flavours – are brought
together in the salads of France, Italy,
Greece and north Africa.

panzanella with radish sandwiches

4 slices white bread (180g), crusts removed
20g butter, softened
4 red radishes (140g), trimmed, sliced thinly
1 medium avocado (250g), halved, chopped coarsely
400g can butter beans, rinsed, drained
4 medium tomatoes (600g), chopped coarsely
1 medium yellow capsicum (200g), chopped coarsely
2 lebanese cucumbers (260g), chopped coarsely
1 cup firmly packed fresh basil leaves

tomato dressing
1 large tomato (220g), peeled, seeded
¼ cup (60ml) olive oil
1 tablespoon white balsamic vinegar
½ teaspoon caster sugar

1 Spread bread with butter; top two slices with radish, top with remaining bread. Using rolling pin, gently flatten radish sandwiches. Cut sandwiches into small squares.

2 Make tomato dressing.

3 Combine avocado and remaining ingredients with the dressing in large bowl. Divide salad among serving plates; top with radish sandwiches.

tomato dressing Blend or process tomato until smooth. Add remaining ingredients; pulse until combined.

prep time *30 minutes* **serves** *8*
nutritional count per serving *14.4g total fat (3.5g saturated fat); 807kJ (193 cal); 10.6g carbohydrate; 4g protein; 3.5g fibre*

To peel the tomato for the dressing, cut a shallow cross in the bottom of the tomato and put it into a bowl of just-boiled water for about 1 minute. The skin should then peel away easily. Cut the peeled tomato in half, then scoop out the seeds using a teaspoon.

char-grilled vegetable salad

1 medium red capsicum (200g)
1 medium yellow capsicum (200g)
1 large red onion (300g), halved, cut into wedges
1 small kumara (250g), sliced thinly lengthways
2 baby eggplants (120g), sliced thinly lengthways
2 medium zucchini (240g), halved lengthways
340g jar artichoke hearts, drained, halved
100g seeded kalamata olives
1 small radicchio (150g), trimmed, leaves separated

oregano dressing
¼ cup (60ml) olive oil
2 tablespoons red wine vinegar
2 tablespoons lemon juice
2 cloves garlic, crushed
1 tablespoon finely chopped fresh oregano leaves

1 Quarter capsicums, remove and discard seeds and membranes; cut capsicum into thick strips.

2 Place ingredients for oregano dressing in screw-top jar; shake well.

3 Cook capsicum, in batches, on heated oiled grill plate (or grill or barbecue) until browned and tender. Cook onion, kumara, eggplant, zucchini and artichoke, in batches, on grill plate until browned.

4 Place char-grilled vegetables, olives and dressing in large bowl; toss gently to combine. Serve vegetables with radicchio.

prep & cook time *55 minutes* **serves** *4*
nutritional per serving *14.8g total fat (2g saturated fat); 1104kJ (264 cal); 22.8g carbohydrate; 6.4g protein; 7.6g fibre*

char-grilled vegetable salad

tomato tapenade pasta salad

500g large spiral pasta
250g cherry tomatoes, halved
50g baby rocket leaves
⅓ cup (25g) shaved parmesan cheese

tomato tapenade
½ cup (75g) drained semi-dried tomatoes in oil
½ cup (60g) seeded black olives
2 tablespoons olive oil
1 tablespoon red wine vinegar
2 teaspoons brown sugar

1 Cook pasta in large saucepan of boiling water until tender; drain. Rinse under cold water; drain.

2 Meanwhile, make tomato tapenade.

3 Place pasta and tapenade in large bowl with remaining ingredients; toss gently to combine.

tomato tapenade Blend or process ingredients until smooth.

prep & cook time *20 minutes* serves *6*
nutritional count per serving *9.5g total fat (2g saturated fat); 1722kJ (412 cal); 65.5g carbohydrate; 12.8g protein; 5.4g fibre*

carpaccio with parmesan

400g piece beef fillet, trimmed
1 baby cos lettuce, trimmed, shredded finely
40g parmesan cheese, shaved finely

basil salsa verde
½ cup finely chopped fresh flat-leaf parsley
¼ cup finely chopped fresh basil
2 tablespoons finely chopped fresh mint
4 drained anchovy fillets, chopped finely
1 tablespoon drained capers, rinsed, chopped finely
1 clove garlic, crushed
2 teaspoons dijon mustard
2 tablespoons red wine vinegar
⅓ cup (80ml) olive oil

1 Enclose beef tightly in plastic wrap; freeze about 1 hour or until partially frozen. Slice beef as thinly as possible.

2 Combine ingredients for basil salsa verde in small bowl.

3 Arrange beef on serving plates in a single layer; top with lettuce and cheese. Spoon salsa verde over beef.

prep time *30 minutes (+ freezing)* serves *6*
nutritional count per serving *18.7g total fat (4.8g saturated fat); 1028kJ (246 cal); 1g carbohydrate; 18g protein; 1.3g fibre*

tomato tapenade pasta salad

carpaccio with parmesan

italian-style bean salad with mozzarella

200g green beans, trimmed, halved crossways
2 x 420g cans four-bean mix, rinsed, drained
2 teaspoons finely chopped fresh thyme
2 teaspoons finely chopped fresh oregano
⅓ cup coarsely chopped fresh flat-leaf parsley
100g mozzarella cheese, sliced thickly
¾ cup (110g) drained sun-dried tomatoes, sliced thinly
1 medium brown onion (150g), sliced thinly
1 cup (120g) seeded black olives

italian dressing
1 clove garlic, crushed
2 tablespoons olive oil
2 tablespoons lemon juice

1 Place ingredients for italian dressing in screw-top jar; shake well.

2 Boil, steam or microwave green beans until tender; drain. Rinse under cold water; drain.

3 Place green beans and four-bean mix in medium bowl with remaining ingredients and dressing; toss gently to combine.

prep & cook time *20 minutes* serves *4*
nutritional count per serving *16.6g total fat (5.1g saturated fat); 1438kJ (344 cal); 28g carbohydrate; 15.6g protein; 10.5g fibre*

greek salad with marinated fetta

2 medium tomatoes (300g)
1 lebanese cucumber (130g)
1 small red capsicum (150g)
1 small red onion (100g), sliced thinly
1 cup (120g) seeded black olives

marinated fetta cheese
200g fetta cheese, cut into 1cm pieces
1 fresh long red chilli, chopped finely
2 teaspoons finely grated lemon rind
2 tablespoons fresh oregano leaves
1 cup (250ml) olive oil

1 Make marinated fetta cheese.

2 Halve and seed tomatoes, cucumber and capsicum; cut vegetables into matchsticks.

3 Place a third of the marinated fetta and a third of the oil marinade in large bowl with tomato, cucumber, capsicum, onion and olives; toss gently to combine.

marinated fetta cheese Place cheese in sterilised jar. Combine remaining ingredients in small jug; pour over cheese. Refrigerate 3 hours or overnight.

prep time *25 minutes (+ refrigeration)* serves *6*
nutritional count per serving *46g total fat (10.5g saturated fat); 1969kJ (471 cal); 7.7g carbohydrate; 7.3g protein; 1.4g fibre*

The remaining marinated fetta can be stored, in the refrigerator, for up to four weeks.

greek-style wild rice salad

2 cups (400g) wild rice blend
1 medium red capsicum (200g)
1 medium brown onion (150g), quartered
250g cherry tomatoes
350g broccolini, halved crossways
½ cup (80g) roasted pine nuts
1 cup coarsely chopped fresh flat-leaf parsley
2 tablespoons lemon juice

lemon and garlic yogurt
2 cloves garlic, crushed
300g yogurt
¼ cup (60ml) lemon juice

1 Combine ingredients for lemon and garlic yogurt in small bowl.

2 Cook rice in large saucepan of boiling water, uncovered, until tender; drain. Place in large serving bowl.

3 Quarter capsicum; discard seeds and membranes. Cook capsicum, onion and tomatoes on heated, oiled grill plate (or grill or barbecue) until tender. Chop capsicum and onion coarsely.

4 Boil, steam or microwave broccolini until tender.

5 Add capsicum, onion and tomatoes to bowl of rice with nuts, parsley and juice; stir gently to combine. Serve salad topped with broccolini, then yogurt.

prep & cook time *35 minutes* serves *4*
nutritional count per serving *11.6g total fat (1.7g saturated fat); 1007kJ (241 cal); 20.2g carbohydrate; 10.9g protein; 6.3g fibre*

greek salad with marinated fetta

greek-style wild rice salad

moussaka salad stacks

2 tablespoons olive oil
1 medium brown onion (150g), chopped finely
2 cloves garlic, crushed
500g beef mince
¼ teaspoon ground cinnamon
½ teaspoon ground nutmeg
2 teaspoons finely grated lemon rind
1 cup (250ml) beef stock
200g fetta cheese, crumbled
½ cup coarsely chopped fresh flat-leaf parsley
1 medium eggplant (300g)
2 medium egg tomatoes (150g), sliced lengthways
20g baby spinach leaves

yogurt dressing
⅔ cup (190g) yogurt
1 tablespoon water
2 teaspoons finely chopped preserved lemon

1 Heat oil in large frying pan; cook onion and garlic, stirring, until onion softens. Add beef, spices and rind; cook, stirring, until beef is cooked through.

2 Add stock to pan; bring to the boil. Reduce heat; simmer, uncovered, about 15 minutes or until liquid is absorbed. Remove from heat; stir in cheese and parsley.

3 Meanwhile, combine ingredients for yogurt dressing in small bowl.

4 Slice eggplant into 10 slices lengthways; discard two skin-side pieces. Cook eggplant and tomato, in batches, on heated oiled grill plate (or grill or barbecue) until browned lightly both sides and tender.

5 Divide half the beef mixture among serving plates, top each with a slice of eggplant, tomato then some of the spinach; drizzle half the dressing over stacks. Repeat making each stack with the remaining ingredients; serve sprinkled with extra parsley leaves, if you like.

prep & cook time *55 minutes*   **serves** *4*
nutritional count per serving *30.2g total fat (13.2g saturated fat); 1973kJ (472 cal); 7.8g carbohydrate; 40.5g protein; 3.5g fibre*

gremolata lamb salad

250g farfalle
600g asparagus, trimmed, halved crossways
200g green beans, trimmed, halved crossways
1 tablespoon vegetable oil
800g lamb backstraps
2 teaspoons dijon mustard
3 shallots (75g), sliced thinly
⅓ cup (50g) roasted pine nuts
⅓ cup loosely packed fresh flat-leaf parsley leaves

lemon dijon dressing
2 tablespoons lemon juice
2 tablespoons extra virgin olive oil
2 teaspoons dijon mustard

gremolata
2 cloves garlic, chopped finely
1 tablespoon finely grated lemon rind
½ cup finely chopped fresh flat-leaf parsley

1   Make lemon dijon dressing and gremolata.

2   Cook pasta in large saucepan of boiling water, uncovered, until just tender; drain. Rinse under cold water; drain.

3   Meanwhile, boil, steam or microwave asparagus and beans, separately, until just tender; drain.

4   Heat oil in large frying pan; cook lamb, uncovered, until browned and cooked as desired. Spread lamb with mustard; press gremolata firmly onto mustard on lamb. Cover; stand 5 minutes. Slice lamb thickly.

5   Place pasta, asparagus, beans and lamb in large bowl with shallots, pine nuts, parsley and dressing; toss gently to combine.

lemon dijon dressing Place ingredients in screw-top jar; shake well.

gremolata Combine ingredients in small bowl.

prep & cook time *40 minutes* serves *4*
nutritional count per serving *41.2g total fat (10.5g saturated fat); 3315kJ (793 cal); 47.4g carbohydrate; 55g protein; 7.1g fibre*

ratatouille & lamb salad

5 baby eggplants (300g), sliced thickly
2 medium zucchini (240g), sliced thickly
1 medium red onion (170g), halved, cut into wedges
1 large red capsicum (350g), cut into 2cm pieces
1 large yellow capsicum (350g), cut into 2cm pieces
250g grape tomatoes
2 cloves garlic, crushed
2 tablespoons olive oil
800g lamb backstraps
1 cup loosely packed fresh basil leaves
150g firm goats cheese, crumbled

pesto dressing
2 cloves garlic, crushed
2 tablespoons finely grated parmesan cheese
1 tablespoon roasted pine nuts
1 tablespoon lemon juice
½ cup firmly packed fresh basil leaves
½ cup (125ml) olive oil

1   Preheat oven to 240°C/220°C fan-forced. Oil two large shallow baking dishes.

2   Divide combined eggplant, zucchini, onion, capsicums, tomatoes, garlic and oil between dishes. Roast, uncovered, about 20 minutes or until tender, stirring occasionally.

3   Meanwhile, make pesto dressing.

4   Cook lamb in heated large non-stick frying pan until browned and cooked as desired. Cover; stand 5 minutes. Slice lamb thickly.

5   Place vegetables in large bowl with basil and cheese; toss gently to combine. Divide vegetables among serving plates; top with lamb, drizzle with dressing.

pesto dressing Blend or process ingredients until smooth.

prep & cook time *55 minutes* serves *4*
nutritional count per serving *55.2g total fat (13.3g saturated fat); 3202kJ (766 cal); 12.6g carbohydrate; 52.9g protein; 6.8g fibre*

gremolata lamb salad

ratatouille & lamb salad

spicy sardines with orange & olive salad

24 butterflied sardines (1kg)
1 clove garlic, crushed
1 tablespoon olive oil
2 tablespoons orange juice
1 teaspoon hot paprika
1 teaspoon finely chopped fresh oregano

orange and olive salad
2 medium oranges (480g)
⅓ cup (40g) seeded black olives, chopped coarsely
50g baby rocket leaves
1 fresh long red chilli, sliced thinly
1 tablespoon orange juice
½ teaspoon finely chopped fresh oregano
1 tablespoon olive oil

1 Place sardines in medium bowl with remaining ingredients; mix gently.

2 Make orange and olive salad.

3 Cook sardines, in batches, on heated oiled grill plate (or grill or barbecue) until browned both sides and cooked through.

4 Divide sardines among plates; serve with salad.

orange and olive salad Peel then segment oranges over medium bowl, add remaining ingredients; toss gently to combine.

prep & cook time *35 minutes* serves *4*
nutritional count per serving *36.2g total fat (8.3g saturated fat); 2500kJ (598 cal); 11.5g carbohydrate; 56g protein; 2.2g fibre*

italian brown rice salad

white beans & olives with rocket

italian brown rice salad

3 cups (750ml) vegetable stock
2 teaspoons olive oil
1 small brown onion (80g), chopped finely
1½ cups (300g) brown medium-grain rice
1 teaspoon finely grated lime rind
1 clove garlic, crushed
⅓ cup (45g) roasted slivered almonds
⅔ cup (100g) sun-dried tomatoes, chopped coarsely
½ cup (60g) seeded black olives, chopped coarsely
½ cup coarsely chopped fresh basil
¼ cup coarsely chopped fresh flat-leaf parsley

lime and mustard dressing
2 tablespoons lime juice
2 tablespoons white wine vinegar
2 cloves garlic, crushed
2 teaspoons dijon mustard

1 Place stock in medium saucepan; bring to the boil. Reduce heat; simmer, covered.

2 Meanwhile, heat oil in large saucepan; cook onion, stirring, until soft. Add rice, rind and garlic; stir to coat rice in onion mixture.

3 Add stock; bring to the boil. Reduce heat; simmer, covered, about 50 minutes or until rice is tender and liquid is absorbed.

4 Place ingredients for lime and mustard dressing in screw-top jar; shake well.

5 Add remaining ingredients and dressing to rice mixture in pan; toss gently to combine.

6 Serve salad warm; top with fresh flat-leaf parsley, if you like.

prep & cook time *1 hour 15 minutes* serves *4*
nutritional count per serving *13.3 g total fat (1.8g saturated fat); 1923kJ (460 cal); 76.3g carbohydrate; 14.7g protein; 9.4g fibre*

white beans & olives with rocket

2 x 400g cans white beans, rinsed, drained
1 medium red onion (170g), chopped finely
⅔ cup (100g) drained semi-dried tomatoes
150g mozzarella cheese, cut into 1cm pieces
½ cup (75g) seeded kalamata olives
150g rocket

oregano balsamic vinaigrette
1 clove garlic, crushed
1 tablespoon finely chopped fresh oregano
¼ cup (60ml) balsamic vinegar
¼ cup (60ml) extra virgin olive oil

1 Place ingredients for oregano balsamic vinaigrette in screw-top jar; shake well.

2 Place beans, onion, tomato, cheese and olives in medium bowl with vinaigrette; toss gently to combine.

3 Serve bean mixture with rocket.

prep time *20 minutes* serves *4*
nutritional count per serving *23.8g total fat (7.4g saturated fat); 1835kJ (439 cal); 29.6g carbohydrate; 21.4g protein; 11.4g fibre*

seafood salads

prawns & tequila mayonnaise, page 216

Seafood salads are perhaps the most popular of all. From canned tuna and salmon to prawns, smoked trout, crab, squid, fresh salmon and smoked salmon, there's nothing that's quite so fresh and so luxurious.

prawns & tequila mayonnaise

900g cooked medium king prawns
¼ cup (75g) mayonnaise
1 tablespoon tequila
juice of 1 lime
1 tablespoon finely chopped fresh chives
3 red witlof (375g)

1   Shell and devein prawns. Chop prawn meat coarsely. Combine prawn meat with mayonnaise, tequila, juice and chives in medium bowl.

2   Trim end from each witlof; separate leaves (you need 24 leaves). Place one level tablespoon of the prawn mixture on each leaf.

prep time 20 minutes   makes 24
nutritional count per witlof leaf 1.1g total fat (0.1g saturated fat); 130kJ (31 cal); 0.7g carbohydrate; 4g protein; 0.3g fibre

warm squid & tomato salad

1 cup (120g) seeded black olives, chopped coarsely
400g fetta cheese, crumbled
1 tablespoon finely grated lemon rind
½ cup loosely packed fresh oregano leaves
12 cleaned small squid hoods (700g)
4 medium egg tomatoes (300g), quartered
1 large red onion (300g), cut into wedges
2 tablespoons olive oil
1 baby endive (300g), trimmed

oregano and red wine dressing
¼ cup (60ml) olive oil
2 tablespoons red wine vinegar
1 clove garlic, crushed
1 tablespoon finely chopped fresh oregano

1   Preheat oven to 180°C/160°C fan-forced.

2   Combine olives, cheese, rind and oregano in small bowl; push cheese mixture into squid hoods. Secure with toothpicks; refrigerate until required.

3   Place tomato and onion in large baking dish; drizzle with oil. Roast about 15 minutes or until tomato begins to soften. Remove dish from oven. Place squid on top of tomato mixture. Roast about 10 minutes or until squid are cooked through.

4   Meanwhile, place ingredients for oregano and red wine dressing in screw-top jar; shake well.

5   Place tomato, onion and endive in large bowl; toss gently to combine. Divide salad among serving plates. Top with squid; drizzle with dressing.

prep & cook time 45 minutes   serves 4
nutritional count per serving 48.8g total fat (19.3g saturated fat); 2913kJ (697 cal); 13.2g carbohydrate; 50.2g protein; 4.3g fibre

warm squid & tomato salad

smoked trout & peach salad

600g piece hot-smoked ocean trout
200g watercress, trimmed
2 medium peaches (460g), cut into thin wedges

lemon buttermilk dressing
¼ cup (60ml) buttermilk
1 tablespoon lemon juice
1 teaspoon finely grated lemon rind
1 teaspoon white sugar

1 Place ingredients for lemon buttermilk dressing in screw-top jar; shake well.

2 Discard skin and bones from fish; break fish into large pieces in medium bowl. Add watercress and peach; toss gently to combine.

3 Serve salad drizzled with dressing.

prep time *10 minutes* serves *4*
nutritional count per serving *8.1g total fat (2g saturated fat); 1170kJ (280 cal); 8.7g carbohydrate; 40.7g protein; 3.3g fibre*

tuna tartare on baby cos

200g piece sashimi tuna, trimmed
1 tablespoon drained capers, rinsed, chopped finely
2 teaspoons prepared horseradish
⅓ cup (80ml) lime juice
2 small tomatoes (180g), seeded, chopped finely
1 small avocado (200g), chopped finely
1 small red onion (100g), chopped finely
1 baby cos lettuce, trimmed, leaves separated
1 tablespoon extra virgin olive oil

1 Cut tuna into 5mm pieces, place in medium bowl with capers, horseradish and 1 tablespoon of the juice; toss gently. Cover; refrigerate 30 minutes.

2 Place tomato, avocado, onion and remaining juice in medium bowl; toss gently to combine.

3 Serve lettuce leaves topped with tomato mixture and tuna tartare, drizzled with oil.

prep time *25 minutes (+ refrigeration time)* serves *6*
nutritional count per serving *10.4g total fat (2.3g saturated fat); 610kJ (146 cal); 2.4g carbohydrate; 9.8g protein; 1.6g fibre*

smoked trout & peach salad

tuna tartare on baby cos

tuna salad

425g can tuna in brine, drained, flaked
1 small red capsicum (150g), chopped finely
2 green onions, sliced thinly
1 trimmed celery stalk (100g), chopped finely
¼ cup finely chopped fresh flat-leaf parsley
2 tablespoons finely chopped fresh basil
2 tablespoons finely chopped fresh dill
½ cup (150g) whole-egg mayonnaise
1 teaspoon dijon mustard
1 teaspoon finely grated lemon rind
2 teaspoons lemon juice

1 Combine tuna, capsicum, onions, celery and herbs in medium bowl.

2 Combine mayonnaise with remaining ingredients in small bowl.

3 Stir mayonnaise mixture into tuna mixture to combine.

prep time *20 minutes* serves *4*
nutritional count per serving *30.1g total fat (4.4g saturated fat); 1547kJ (370 cal); 2.1g carbohydrate; 23g protein; 1.4g fibre*

potato, tuna & broad bean salad

10 small potatoes (1.2kg), sliced thickly
¼ cup (60ml) olive oil
2 tablespoons wholegrain mustard
1 tablespoon white wine vinegar
2 tablespoons lemon juice
½ small red onion (50g), sliced thinly
425g tuna in springwater, drained, flaked
500g frozen broad beans

1 Boil, steam or microwave potato until tender; drain.

2 Whisk oil, mustard, vinegar and juice in small bowl.

3 Combine potato in large bowl with dressing, onion and tuna.

4 Meanwhile, boil, steam or microwave beans until just tender. Peel; add to potato salad. Toss gently to serve.

prep & cook time *30 minutes* serves *4*
nutritional count per serving *16.7g total fat (2.8g saturated fat); 2190kJ (524 cal); 49.9g carbohydrate; 35.2g protein; 15.7g fibre*

salmon & grapefruit salad

180g salmon fillet
1 tablespoon lemon juice
1cm piece fresh ginger (5g), grated
½ teaspoon ground cumin
2 ruby red grapefruits (700g)
1 tablespoon white balsamic vinegar
½ teaspoon white sugar
80g baby spinach leaves
1½ cups (120g) bean sprouts
1 lebanese cucumber (130g), seeded, sliced thinly

1 Combine fish in medium bowl with juice, ginger and cumin. Cook fish in small baking-paper-lined steamer, over small saucepan of simmering water, about 10 minutes. Using two forks, flake fish.

2 Meanwhile, segment grapefruits over small bowl; reserve ⅓ cup of the juice for dressing. To make dressing, place reserved juice, vinegar and sugar in screw-top jar; shake well.

3 Divide spinach, sprouts, cucumber and grapefruit segments among serving plates; top with flaked salmon and dressing.

prep & cook time *20 minutes* serves *4*
nutritional count per serving *3.5g total fat (0.7g saturated fat); 456kJ (109 cal); 6.7g carbohydrate; 11.3g protein; 2.4g fibre*

potato, tuna & broad bean salad

salmon & grapefruit salad

crab & fennel salad

4 uncooked blue swimmer crabs (1.5kg)
10cm stick fresh lemon grass (20g), cut lengthways
4cm piece fresh ginger (20g), sliced thickly
½ cup loosely packed fresh coriander leaves
½ cup loosely packed fresh basil leaves

fennel salad
2 medium oranges (480g)
1 large fennel bulb (550g)
1 tablespoon rice vinegar
2 teaspoons olive oil
1 small radicchio (150g), leaves separated, torn
¼ cup loosely packed fresh chervil leaves

1 Lift flap under body of each crab; turn crab over, hold body with one hand while pulling off top part of shell with the other. Discard shell and gills on either side of body. Rinse crab under cold water; chop body in half.

2 Place lemon grass, ginger and herbs in large baking-paper-lined steamer, over large saucepan of simmering water; top with crab. Cook about 10 minutes or until crab is changed in colour.

3 Meanwhile, make fennel salad.

4 Serve crab with fennel salad.

fennel salad Segment oranges over small bowl; reserve juice. Using mandolin or V-slicer, cut fennel into paper-thin slices. Combine fennel, reserved juice, vinegar and oil in large bowl. Add radicchio, chervil and orange segments; toss gently to combine.

prep & cook time *20 minutes* serves *4*
nutritional count per serving *3.2g total fat (0.4g saturated fat); 589kJ (141 cal); 11.2g carbohydrate; 14.2g protein; 5.1g fibre*

crab & green mango salad

125g bean thread noodles
2 green mangoes (700g), cut into matchsticks
300g cooked crab meat, flaked
1 small red onion (100g), sliced thinly
100g baby mizuna leaves
1 cup firmly packed fresh coriander leaves

sweet chilli dressing
⅓ cup (80ml) lime juice
2 tablespoons fish sauce
2 tablespoons sweet chilli sauce
1 tablespoon grated palm sugar

1 Place noodles in medium heatproof bowl, cover with boiling water; stand until almost tender, drain. Rinse under cold water; drain.

2 Meanwhile, place ingredients for sweet chilli dressing in screw-top jar; shake well.

3 Place noodles and dressing in large bowl with remaining ingredients; toss gently to combine.

prep & cook time *20 minutes*   serves *4*
nutritional count per serving *1.4g total fat (0.1g saturated fat); 953kJ (228 cal); 37.2g carbohydrate; 14g protein; 3.9g fibre*

cajun fish salad with asian greens

1 tablespoon cajun spice mix
½ teaspoon sea salt flakes
2 x 200g firm white fish fillets
cooking-oil spray
2 lebanese cucumbers (260g), seeded, sliced thinly
150g sugar snap peas, trimmed, halved lengthways
100g baby asian greens
1 cup loosely packed fresh coriander leaves
½ cup loosely packed fresh mint leaves
1 green onion, sliced thinly

yogurt dressing
½ cup (140g) low-fat natural yogurt
2 tablespoons lemon juice

1 Combine spice and salt in medium shallow bowl, add fish; coat in spice mixture.

2 Spray heated medium frying pan with cooking-oil spray for 1 second; cook fish, over medium heat, about 5 minutes each side or until cooked through. Cover; stand 5 minutes. Using two forks, flake fish into chunks.

3 Meanwhile, combine ingredients for yogurt dressing in small bowl.

4 Place cucumber, peas, asian greens, herbs and onion in large bowl; toss gently to combine. Serve salad topped with flaked fish; drizzle with dressing.

prep & cook time *25 minutes*   serves *4*
nutritional count per serving *5g total fat (1.5g saturated fat); 1070kJ (256 cal); 5.8g carbohydrate; 45g protein; 2.7g fibre*

barbecued octopus salad

600g baby octopus
1 teaspoon finely grated lemon rind
2 tablespoons lemon juice
2 teaspoons finely chopped fresh oregano
1 clove garlic, crushed
½ teaspoon cracked black pepper
cooking-oil spray

tomato salad
4 medium tomatoes (600g), seeded, chopped coarsely
2 lebanese cucumbers (260g), chopped coarsely
1 small red onion (100g), chopped finely
1 small green capsicum (150g), chopped coarsely
1 tablespoon coarsely chopped fresh oregano leaves
1 tablespoon white wine vinegar

1 Toss ingredients for tomato salad in medium bowl.

2 Combine octopus, rind, juice, oregano, garlic and pepper in medium bowl.

3 Spray heated barbecue grill plate with cooking-oil spray for 2 seconds. Cook octopus, turning occasionally, until cooked through.

4 Serve octopus with tomato salad, and lemon wedges, if you like.

prep & cook time *25 minutes*   serves *4*
nutritional count per serving *1.9g total fat (0g saturated fat); 681kJ (163 cal); 6.9g carbohydrate; 27.4g protein; 3.4g fibre*

cajun fish salad with asian greens

barbecued octopus salad

salmon with fennel & beetroot salad

1 small fennel bulb (200g), trimmed
1 medium beetroot (175g), peeled
1 small radicchio (150g), trimmed, shredded finely
½ cup loosely packed fresh flat-leaf parsley leaves
1 tablespoon rice wine vinegar
¼ cup (60ml) olive oil
4 salmon fillets (880g)
1½ teaspoons caraway seeds
1 clove garlic, crushed
1 lime, cut into wedges

1 Using mandolin, V-slicer or very sharp knife, slice fennel and beetroot finely. Place in large bowl with radicchio, parsley, vinegar and 2 tablespoons of the oil; toss gently to combine.

2 Combine fish, remaining oil, seeds and garlic in large bowl. Cook fish in heated large frying pan until cooked as desired.

3 Divide salad and fish among serving plates; serve with lime.

prep & cook time *30 minutes* serves 4
nutritional count per serving *29.5g total fat (5.5g saturated fat); 1960kJ (469 cal); 4.8g carbohydrate; 44.7g protein; 3.6g fibre*

mango & prawn salad

1kg uncooked medium king prawns
2 tablespoons light soy sauce
2 teaspoons sesame oil
1 fresh long red chilli, chopped finely
2 teaspoons finely chopped fresh coriander
    root and stem mixture
1cm piece fresh ginger (5g), grated
2 cloves garlic, crushed
1 medium mango (430g), sliced thinly
1 large red capsicum (350g), sliced thinly
1 lebanese cucumber (130g), seeded, sliced thinly
1 cup (80g) bean sprouts
½ cup loosely packed fresh coriander leaves
2 green onions, sliced thinly

lime dressing
⅓ cup (80ml) lime juice
1 tablespoon grated palm sugar
2 teaspoons fish sauce

1 Shell and devein prawns, leaving tails intact. Combine prawns in medium bowl with sauce, oil, chilli, root and stem mixture, ginger and garlic. Refrigerate 30 minutes.

2 Meanwhile, place ingredients for lime dressing in screw-top jar; shake well.

3 Cook prawns in heated large frying pan, in batches, until changed in colour.

4 Combine prawns, dressing and remaining ingredients in large bowl.

prep and cook time *35 minutes (+ refrigeration)* serves 4
nutritional count per serving *3.5g total fat (0.5g saturated fat); 970kJ (232 cal); 18g carbohydrate; 29.7g protein; 3.6g fibre*

salmon with fennel & beetroot salad

mango & prawn salad

smoked salmon, orange & avocado salad

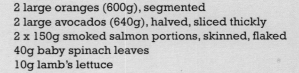

2 large oranges (600g), segmented
2 large avocados (640g), halved, sliced thickly
2 x 150g smoked salmon portions, skinned, flaked
40g baby spinach leaves
10g lamb's lettuce

horseradish cream dressing
¼ cup (60ml) orange juice
1 tablespoon olive oil
1 tablespoon white wine vinegar
1 tablespoon horseradish cream

1 Place ingredients for horseradish cream dressing in screw-top jar; shake well.

2 Place orange, avocado, fish, spinach and lettuce in large bowl; toss gently to combine. Divide salad among serving plates; drizzle with dressing.

prep time *15 minutes* serves *4*
nutritional count per serving *35.9g total fat (7.7g saturated fat); 1856kJ (444 cal); 10.9g carbohydrate; 18.3g protein; 4.3g fibre*

snow pea, prawn & avocado salad

750g cooked medium king prawns
150g sugar snap peas, trimmed
3 small avocados (600g), sliced thickly
2 cups (100g) snow pea sprouts

chive vinaigrette
¼ cup (60ml) white wine vinegar
¼ cup (60ml) olive oil
¼ cup finely chopped fresh chives

1 Combine ingredients for chive vinaigrette in small bowl.

2 Shell and devein prawns, leaving tails intact.

3 Boil, steam or microwave peas until just tender; rinse under cold water, drain.

4 Place peas in large bowl with prawns, avocado, sprouts and vinaigrette; toss gently to combine.

prep & cook time *25 minutes* serves *4*
nutritional count per serving *38.2g total fat (7.2g saturated fat); 1998kJ (478 cal); 8.2g carbohydrate; 24.6g protein; 3.7g fibre*

rösti stacks with prawns

16 uncooked medium king prawns (720g)
800g russet burbank potatoes, grated coarsely
1 teaspoon finely chopped fresh rosemary
2 cloves garlic, crushed
2 tablespoons olive oil
30g baby rocket leaves

mint aïoli
⅓ cup coarsely chopped fresh mint
1 clove garlic, quartered
1 egg
1 tablespoon dijon mustard
½ cup (125ml) olive oil

1 Make mint aïoli.

2 Shell and devein prawns, leaving tails intact.

3 To make rösti, squeeze excess moisture from potato; combine in medium bowl with rosemary and garlic. Divide into eight portions.

4 Heat half the oil in large frying pan; cook rösti, in batches, flattening slightly, until browned both sides. Drain.

5 Heat remaining oil in pan; cook prawns until just changed in colour.

6 Serve rösti stacked alternately with prawns, mint aïoli and rocket.

mint aïoli Blend or process mint, garlic, egg and mustard until mixture is pureed. With motor operating, add oil in a thin, steady stream until mixture thickens.

prep & cook time *50 minutes* serves *4*
nutritional count per serving *39.8g total fat (5.8g saturated fat); 2324kJ (556 cal); 23.6g carbohydrate; 24.9g protein; 3.7g fibre*

snow pea, prawn & avocado salad

rösti stacks with prawns

coriander & chilli-marinated seafood salad

1kg uncooked large king prawns
600g cleaned baby octopus, halved lengthways
400g piece salmon fillet, skin on
400g squid hoods, cleaned, cut into rings
16 scallops (400g), roe removed
16 small black mussels (400g)
200g rocket
250g cherry tomatoes, halved
2 large avocados (640g), sliced thickly
1 cup loosely packed fresh coriander leaves

coriander and chilli marinade
4 coriander roots
¼ cup loosely packed fresh coriander leaves
2 cloves garlic, crushed
1 small red onion (100g), chopped coarsely
2 fresh small red thai chillies, chopped coarsely
3 fresh long red chillies, chopped coarsely
¼ cup (60ml) red wine vinegar
½ cup (125ml) olive oil
⅓ cup (80ml) lime juice
1 teaspoon sugar

lime dressing
2 tablespoons lime juice
¼ cup (60ml) peanut oil

1 Make coriander and chilli marinade.

2 Shell and devein prawns, leaving tails intact. Place prawns in large bowl with octopus, salmon, squid, scallops and marinade; toss gently to combine. Cover; refrigerate 3 hours or overnight.

3 Cook marinated seafood, in batches, on heated oiled grill plate (or grill or barbecue) until browned all over and cooked as desired. Flake salmon into large pieces.

4 Meanwhile, scrub mussels; remove beards. Cook mussels, covered, on same heated oiled grill plate until mussels open (discard any that do not).

5 Make lime dressing.

6 Place seafood in large bowl with rocket, tomato, avocado, coriander and dressing; toss gently to combine.

coriander and chilli marinade Blend or process ingredients until combined.

lime dressing Place ingredients in screw-top jar; shake well.

prep & cook time *55 minutes (+ refrigeration)* serves *8* nutritional count per serving *30.2g total fat (13.2g saturated fat); 1973kJ (472 cal); 7.8g carbohydrate; 40.5g protein; 3.5g fibre*

char-grilled scallop salad

2 red witlof (250g), quartered
16 scallops (400g) roe removed

orange dressing
2 tablespoons olive oil
1 tablespoon orange juice

orange gremolata
¼ cup finely chopped fresh flat-leaf parsley
1 tablespoon finely grated orange rind
1 clove garlic, crushed

1 Combine ingredients for orange dressing in small jug.

2 Combine ingredients for orange gremolata in small bowl.

3 Cook witlof on heated oiled grill plate (or grill or barbecue) until browned lightly.

4 Cook scallops on grill plate until cooked.

5 Drizzle witlof and scallops with dressing and serve accompanied with gremolata.

prep & cook time *20 minutes* serves *4*
nutritional count per serving *9.9g total fat (1.5g saturated fat); 615kJ (147 cal); 1.7g carbohydrate; 12.3g protein; 1.4g fibre*

char-grilled chilli squid salad

800g cleaned squid hoods
450g fresh wide rice noodles
1 medium red capsicum (200g), sliced thinly
150g snow peas, trimmed, halved
1 lebanese cucumber (130g), seeded, sliced thinly
1 small red onion (100g), sliced thinly
1 cup loosely packed fresh coriander leaves
⅓ cup coarsely chopped fresh mint

sweet chilli dressing
½ cup (125ml) water
⅓ cup (75g) caster sugar
1 tablespoon white vinegar
2 fresh small red thai chillies, chopped finely

1 Cut squid down centre to open out; score the inside in a diagonal pattern. Halve squid lengthways; cut squid into 3cm pieces.

2 Make sweet chilli dressing.

3 Cook squid on heated oiled grill plate (or grill or barbecue), in batches, until tender and browned.

4 Place noodles in large heatproof bowl, cover with boiling water; separate with fork, drain. Combine noodles in large serving bowl with squid, dressing and remaining ingredients.

sweet chilli dressing Stir the water and sugar in small saucepan, over low heat, until sugar dissolves; bring to the boil. Reduce heat; simmer, uncovered, without stirring, about 5 minutes or until syrup thickens slightly. Stir in vinegar and chilli off the heat.

prep & cook time *30 minutes* serves *4*
nutritional count per serving *3.1g total fat (0.8g saturated fat); 1584kJ (379 cal); 48.3g carbohydrate; 38.1g protein; 2.8g fibre*

char-grilled scallop salad

char-grilled chilli squid salad

poached trout & potato salad

grilled balmain bug salad

poached trout & potato salad

800g kipfler potatoes, unpeeled, halved
1 litre (4 cups) water
4 x 5cm strips lemon rind
2 sprigs fresh dill
600g ocean trout fillets
1 small red onion (100g), sliced thinly
1 lebanese cucumber (130g), seeded, sliced thinly
50g rocket leaves

lemon and dill dressing
⅓ cup (80ml) olive oil
¼ cup (60ml) lemon juice
1 clove garlic, crushed
1 tablespoon finely chopped fresh dill
1 tablespoon drained baby capers, rinsed

1 Boil, steam or microwave potato until tender; drain.

2 Place the water, rind and dill in medium saucepan; bring to the boil. Add fish; simmer, covered, about 10 minutes or until cooked as desired. Drain fish; discard cooking liquid. Flake fish coarsely into large bowl; discard skin.

3 Meanwhile, place ingredients for lemon and dill dressing in screw-top jar; shake well.

4 Add potato, dressing and remaining ingredients to bowl with fish; toss gently to combine.

prep & cook time *25 minutes* **serves** *4*
nutritional count per serving *24.3g total fat (3.9g saturated fat); 2031kJ (486 cal); 29.3g carbohydrate; 34.9g protein; 5.1g fibre*

grilled balmain bug salad

2 baby eggplants (120g)
1 medium zucchini (120g)
1 medium red capsicum (200g), chopped finely
3 flat mushrooms (240g), quartered
2 tablespoons olive oil
6 uncooked balmain bug tails (1.5kg), halved lengthways
250g rocket, trimmed

chilli lime butter
60g butter, softened
2 teaspoons finely grated lime rind
2 tablespoons lime juice
1 fresh long red chilli, chopped finely
2 cloves garlic, crushed

1 Using vegetable peeler, cut eggplant and zucchini into long, thin strips. Combine eggplant, zucchini, capsicum, mushrooms and oil in large bowl.

2 Cook vegetables, in batches, on heated oiled grill plate (or grill or barbecue) until tender. Cover to keep warm.

3 Cook balmain bugs on heated oiled grill plate until cooked.

4 Meanwhile, combine ingredients for chilli lime butter in small bowl.

5 Place vegetables, balmain bugs and chilli lime butter in large bowl; toss to combine.

6 Divide rocket among serving plates; top with vegetable and balmain bug mixture.

prep & cook time *40 minutes* **serves** *4*
nutritional count per serving *25.1g total fat (10g saturated fat); 2282kJ (456 cal); 5.4g carbohydrate; 72.4g protein; 4.6g fibre*

poultry salads

quail & pear radicchio salad, page 244

Most of the recipes in this chapter are for chicken but there's also quail, duck and turkey. Poultry makes an excellent salad, especially if it's eaten at room temperature rather than fridge-cold.

quail & pear radicchio salad

4 quails (640g)
16 fresh sage leaves
4 slices prosciutto (60g), halved lengthways
2 teaspoons olive oil
1 ruby red grapefruit (350g)
40g butter
2 small pears (360g), cut into wedges
2 small radicchio (300g), trimmed, leaves separated

balsamic dressing
2 tablespoons balsamic vinegar
1 tablespoon olive oil
1 clove garlic, crushed

1 Using kitchen scissors, cut along sides of each quail's backbone; discard backbones. Halve each quail along breastbone. Place 2 sage leaves on each quail half; wrap with slice of prosciutto.

2 Heat oil in large frying pan; cook quail, in batches, about 10 minutes or until cooked.

3 Meanwhile, segment grapefruit over small bowl; reserve 1 tablespoon of juice for dressing.

4 Make balsamic dressing.

5 Heat butter in medium frying pan; add pear, cook about 4 minutes or until tender.

6 Divide radicchio, grapefruit and pear among serving plates; top with quail, drizzle with dressing.

balsamic dressing Place vinegar, oil, garlic and reserved grapefruit juice in screw-top jar; shake well.

prep & cook time *45 minutes* serves *4*
nutritional count per serving *25.1g total fat (9g saturated fat); 1522kJ (364 cal); 13.6g carbohydrate; 19.4g protein; 3.9g fibre*

five-spice duck & peach salad

¼ cup (90g) honey
1 teaspoon five-spice powder
4 medium peaches (600g), quartered
100g snow peas, trimmed, halved on the diagonal
4 duck breast fillets (600g), skin on
1 tablespoon red wine vinegar
2 tablespoons olive oil
1 teaspoon dijon mustard
1 shallot (25g), chopped finely
100g baby spinach leaves

1 Cook honey, five-spice and peaches in large heated frying pan, stirring, about 5 minutes or until peaches are browned lightly. Remove from pan; cover to keep warm.

2 Meanwhile, boil, steam or microwave snow peas until just tender; drain. Rinse under cold water; drain.

3 Score duck skins; cook duck, skin-side down, in same pan, over medium heat, about 10 minutes or until browned and crisp. Turn duck; cook about 5 minutes or until cooked as desired. Remove from pan; cover to keep warm.

4 Combine vinegar, oil, mustard and shallot in large bowl. Add snow peas and spinach; toss gently to combine.

5 Slice duck thinly; serve with peaches and salad.

prep & cook time *30 minutes* serves *4*
nutritional count per serving *17.6g total fat (3.7g saturated fat); 1643kJ (393 cal); 28.2g carbohydrate; 29.4g protein; 3.1g fibre*

five-spice duck & peach salad

turkey, fig & spinach salad

6 large fresh figs (480g), quartered
100g baby spinach leaves
100g shaved turkey breast, chopped coarsely

raspberry dressing
2 tablespoons raspberry vinegar
2 teaspoons walnut oil

1 Place ingredients for raspberry dressing in screw-top jar; shake well.

2 Place figs, spinach, turkey and dressing in large bowl; toss gently to combine.

prep time *10 minutes* serves *4*
nutritional count per serving *3.8g total fat (0.5g saturated fat); 502kJ (120 cal); 9.9g carbohydrate; 9.6g protein; 3.7g fibre*

chicken & cucumber salad

150g chicken breast fillet, sliced thinly
1 clove garlic, crushed
1 tablespoon lemon juice
1 teaspoon finely chopped fresh oregano
¼ teaspoon sweet paprika
2 slices wholemeal lavash bread (120g)
cooking-oil spray

cucumber salad
1 telegraph cucumber (400g), halved lengthways,
    sliced thinly
1 large green capsicum (350g), sliced thinly
4 medium egg tomatoes (300g), seeded, sliced thinly
1 tablespoon coarsely chopped fresh dill
1 tablespoon coarsely chopped fresh oregano
¼ cup (60ml) white wine vinegar
2 teaspoons white sugar

1 Combine chicken, garlic, juice, oregano and paprika in medium bowl. Cover; refrigerate 30 minutes.

2 Meanwhile, preheat grill. Toast bread, both sides; break bread into large pieces.

3 Make cucumber salad.

4 Spray heated medium frying pan with cooking-oil spray for 1 second; cook chicken in pan until cooked through.

5 Add chicken and bread to cucumber salad; toss gently. Serve immediately.

cucumber salad Combine ingredients in large bowl.

prep & cook time *25 minutes (+ refrigeration)* serves 4
nutritional count per serving *2g total fat (0.4g saturated fat); 706kJ (169 cal); 21.8g carbohydrate; 13.2g protein; 4.6g fibre*

chicken coleslaw

3 cups (480g) shredded barbecued chicken
3 cups (240g) finely shredded wombok
3 cups (240g) finely shredded savoy cabbage
3 cups (240g) finely shredded red cabbage
2 medium carrots (240g), grated coarsely
1 medium green capsicum (200g), sliced thinly
¼ cup finely chopped fresh dill

fennel slaw dressing
½ cup (140g) yogurt
⅓ cup (100g) mayonnaise
⅓ cup (80ml) cider vinegar
1 small brown onion (80g), grated coarsely
2 teaspoons white sugar
2 teaspoons fennel seeds

1 Combine ingredients for fennel slaw dressing in small bowl.

2 Place salad ingredients in large bowl with dressing; toss gently to combine. Refrigerate, covered, at least 1 hour.

prep time *25 minutes (+ refrigeration)* serves *6* nutritional count per serving *12.4g total fat (2.9g saturated fat); 1095kJ (262 cal); 11.3g carbohydrate; 23.7g protein; 5g fibre*

chicken rice salad

2 cups (500ml) water
4 x 5cm strips lemon rind
600g chicken breast fillets
3 cups cooked wild rice blend
1 cup thinly sliced fresh mint
½ cup (65g) dried cranberries
2 tablespoons finely chopped preserved lemon rind

lemon cranberry dressing
⅓ cup (80ml) olive oil
¼ cup (60ml) cranberry juice
2 tablespoons lemon juice
2 teaspoons caster sugar
1 tablespoon cranberry sauce

1 Place the water and rind in medium saucepan; bring to the boil. Add chicken; reduce heat. Simmer, covered, about 10 minutes or until chicken is cooked through. Cool chicken in liquid 10 minutes; drain. Slice chicken thinly.

2 Meanwhile, place ingredients for lemon cranberry dressing in screw-top jar; shake well.

3 Place chicken and dressing in large bowl with remaining ingredients; toss gently to combine.

prep & cook time *25 minutes* serves *4* nutritional count per serving *27.1g total fat (5.2g saturated fat); 2646kJ (633 cal); 59.3g carbohydrate; 36.3g protein; 3.2g fibre*

chicken coleslaw

chicken rice salad

tamarind honey chicken with asian wombok salad

¼ cup (60ml) peanut oil
¼ cup (60ml) tamarind concentrate
1 tablespoon honey
2 teaspoons dark soy sauce
½ teaspoon finely grated lime rind
1 tablespoon lime juice
1 clove garlic, crushed
800g chicken breast fillets
½ small wombok (350g), trimmed, shredded finely
4 green onions, sliced thinly
500g red radishes, trimmed, sliced thinly,
    cut into matchsticks
2 lebanese cucumbers (260g), halved widthways,
    seeded, cut into matchsticks
½ cup loosely packed fresh mint leaves
½ cup loosely packed fresh coriander leaves
⅔ cup (50g) fried shallots

honey lime dressing
1 tablespoon honey
2 tablespoons lime juice
1 teaspoon sesame oil
1 tablespoon dark soy sauce
1 fresh long red chilli, chopped finely

1 Combine 1 tablespoon of the oil, tamarind, honey, sauce, rind, juice, garlic and chicken in large bowl, cover; refrigerate 3 hours or overnight.

2 Place ingredients for honey lime dressing in screw-top jar; shake well.

3 Heat remaining oil in large frying pan; cook chicken mixture, in batches, until cooked through. Stand 5 minutes; slice chicken thickly. Cover to keep warm.

4 Meanwhile, place dressing in large bowl with remaining ingredients; toss gently to combine.

5 Divide salad among plates; top with chicken.

prep & cook time *55 minutes (+ refrigeration)* serves 4
nutritional count per serving *27g total fat (6.1g saturated fat); 2144kJ (513 cal); 19.4g carbohydrate; 46.3g protein; 4.3g fibre*

smoked chicken & peach salad

170g asparagus, trimmed, cut into 3cm lengths
600g smoked chicken breast fillets, sliced thinly
1 small red onion (100g), sliced thinly
2 medium peaches (300g), sliced thinly
1 cup (120g) roasted pecans
150g baby spinach leaves

dill vinaigrette
⅓ cup (80ml) olive oil
2 tablespoons cider vinegar
1 tablespoon finely chopped fresh dill

1 Boil, steam or microwave asparagus until tender; drain. Rinse under cold water; drain.

2 Place ingredients for dill vinaigrette in screw-top jar; shake well.

3 Place asparagus and vinaigrette with remaining ingredients in large bowl; toss gently to combine.

prep & cook time *20 minutes* serves *4*
nutritional count per serving *50.5g total fat (6.9g saturated fat); 2750kJ (658 cal); 7.4g carbohydrate; 42.4g protein; 5.2g fibre*

chicken liver, bacon & apple salad

4 rindless bacon rashers (260g), sliced thinly
1 tablespoon olive oil
500g chicken livers, halved, trimmed
200g lamb's lettuce
250g baby spinach leaves
1 medium apple (150g), halved, sliced into thin wedges

cranberry dressing
4 shallots (100g), chopped finely
2 tablespoons red wine vinegar
⅓ cup (80ml) olive oil
¼ cup (80g) whole berry cranberry sauce, warmed

1 Combine ingredients for cranberry dressing in small bowl.

2 Cook bacon, stirring, in large frying pan until crisp; drain on absorbent paper.

3 Heat oil in same clean pan; cook liver, over high heat, about 5 minutes or until browned and cooked as desired (do not overcook or liver will be dry and tasteless). Drain on absorbent paper.

4 Place bacon and liver in large bowl with dressing and remaining ingredients; toss gently to combine.

prep & cook time *30 minutes* serves *4*
nutritional count per serving *33g total fat (6.7g saturated fat); 2027kJ (485 cal); 14.3g carbohydrate; 32.2g protein; 3.5g fibre*

smoked chicken & peach salad

chicken liver, bacon & apple salad

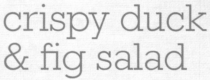

crispy duck & fig salad

600g duck breast fillets, skin on
80g trimmed watercress
250g yellow grape tomatoes, halved
4 medium figs (240g), cut into wedges

spiced balsamic glaze
½ cup (125ml) balsamic vinegar
2 tablespoons brown sugar
½ teaspoon ground cinnamon
¼ teaspoon ground clove

1 Make spiced balsamic glaze.

2 Meanwhile, cook duck, skin-side down, in heated oiled large frying pan about 5 minutes or until skin is crisp. Turn duck; cook about 5 minutes or until cooked as desired. Cover, stand 5 minutes, then slice duck thinly.

3 Place watercress and tomatoes in medium bowl with dressing; toss gently to combine. Divide figs among plates; top with tomato mixture then duck.

spiced balsamic glaze Stir ingredients in small saucepan over low heat, without boiling, until sugar dissolves. Bring to the boil; reduce heat. Simmer, uncovered, about 5 minutes or until syrup thickens slightly. Cool. If glaze becomes too thick, stir in a little boiling water.

prep & cook time *25 minutes* serves *4*
nutritional count per serving *55.6g total fat (16.7g saturated fat); 2650kJ (634 cal); 12.6g carbohydrate; 21g protein; 2.9g fibre*

chicken & kumara salad

2 teaspoons mixed spice
800g chicken breast fillets
1 medium kumara (400g), sliced thinly
1 large red onion (300g), cut into wedges
100g baby rocket leaves

maple dressing
¼ cup (60ml) olive oil
2 tablespoons malt vinegar
2 tablespoons orange juice
1 tablespoon maple syrup
2 teaspoons dijon mustard

1 Place ingredients for maple dressing in screw-top jar; shake well.

2 Rub mixed spice all over chicken; cook chicken on heated oiled grill plate (or grill or barbecue) until cooked. Cover chicken; stand 5 minutes then slice thinly.

3 Meanwhile, cook kumara and onion on heated oiled grill plate until tender.

4 Place chicken, kumara and onion in large bowl with rocket and dressing; toss gently to combine.

prep & cook time *40 minutes* serves *4*
nutritional count per serving *25g total fat (5.3g saturated fat); 2107kJ (504 cal); 21.9g carbohydrate; 46.3g protein; 3g fibre*

chilli quail & mandarin salad

8 whole quails (1.6kg)
4 fresh small red thai chillies, chopped coarsely
2 cloves garlic, halved
¼ cup (60ml) olive oil
2 tablespoons lemon juice
4 medium mandarins (800g)
300g snow peas, trimmed, halved
340g watercress, trimmed
1 cup (160g) roasted blanched almonds
200g seedless red grapes, halved lengthways

1 Using kitchen scissors, cut along both sides of each quail's backbone; discard backbones. Place each quail flat, skin-side down, on chopping board; discard ribcages. Cut each quail into quarters.

2 Blend or process chilli, garlic, oil and half of the lemon juice until smooth; combine with quail pieces in large bowl. Cover; refrigerate 20 minutes.

3 Meanwhile, segment peeled mandarins over large bowl to save juice. Reserve segments with juice.

4 Cook undrained quail on heated oiled grill plate (or grill or barbecue) until browned both sides and cooked through.

5 Meanwhile, boil, steam or microwave peas until just tender; drain.

6 Place quail and peas in large bowl with mandarin segments and juice, watercress, nuts, grapes and remaining lemon juice; toss gently to combine.

prep & cook time *1 hour (+ refrigeration)* serves *4*
nutritional count per serving *58.7g total fat (9.1g saturated fat); 3528kJ (844 cal); 24.4g carbohydrate; 50.9g protein; 10.5g fibre*

chicken & kumara salad

chilli quail & mandarin salad

smoked chicken salad

chicken & wild rice salad

258　poultry salads

smoked chicken salad

2 cups (400g) wild rice blend
200g seedless red grapes
3 trimmed celery stalks (300g), sliced thinly
½ cup (60g) roasted pecans
350g watercress, trimmed
500g smoked chicken breasts, sliced thinly

lime and black pepper dressing
½ cup (125ml) lime juice
½ cup (125ml) olive oil
1 tablespoon caster sugar
¼ teaspoon cracked black pepper

1 Cook rice in large saucepan of boiling water, uncovered, until just tender; drain. Rinse under cold water; drain.

2 Meanwhile, place ingredients for lime and black pepper dressing in screw-top jar; shake well.

3 Place rice in large bowl with grapes, celery, nuts and half of the dressing; toss gently to combine.

4 Divide watercress among serving plates; top with rice salad then chicken. Drizzle with remaining dressing.

prep & cook time *25 minutes* serves *6*
nutritional count per serving *33.9g total fat (5.1g saturated fat); 2851kJ (682 cal); 61.9g carbohydrate; 29.1g protein; 6.4g fibre*

chicken & wild rice salad

1 litre (4 cups) water
800g chicken breast fillets
1½ cups (300g) wild rice blend
⅔ cup (110g) roasted blanched almonds
1 cup (190g) black grapes
¼ cup loosely packed fresh tarragon leaves
2 green onions, sliced finely
2 teaspoons finely grated lemon rind
1 tablespoon lemon juice

tarragon dressing
½ cup (120g) sour cream
1 tablespoon dijon mustard
1 tablespoon finely chopped fresh tarragon
1 tablespoon water
2 teaspoons lemon juice

1 Bring the water to the boil in large frying pan; add chicken. Simmer, covered, about 10 minutes or until chicken is cooked. Cool chicken in poaching liquid 10 minutes; drain, slice thickly.

2 Cook rice in large saucepan of boiling water, uncovered, until tender; drain. Cool 10 minutes.

3 Combine ingredients for tarragon dressing in small bowl.

4 Place rice in large bowl with nuts, grapes, tarragon, onion, rind and juice; toss gently to combine.

5 Serve rice salad topped with chicken, accompanied with dressing.

prep & cook time *45 minutes* serves *4*
nutritional count per serving *32.1g total fat (10g saturated fat); 2575kJ (616 cal); 24.4g carbohydrate; 55.3g protein; 4.5g fibre*

warm duck, apple & walnut salad

2 large granny smith apples (400g),
    unpeeled, quartered, cored
¾ cup (180ml) cider vinegar
¾ cup (180ml) water
1 tablespoon brown sugar
2 x 5cm strips lemon rind
1 cinnamon stick
1 star anise
4 duck breast fillets (600g), skin on
1 teaspoon sea salt flakes
1 teaspoon ground sichuan pepper
¼ teaspoon ground ginger
40g butter
80g baby spinach leaves
4 green onions, cut into 3cm pieces
¼ cup (25g) coarsely chopped walnuts

sweet mustard dressing
2 tablespoons rice vinegar
1 tablespoon olive oil
2 teaspoons mirin
1 teaspoon dijon mustard

1 Place apple, vinegar, the water, sugar, rind, cinnamon and star anise in medium saucepan; bring to the boil. Reduce heat; simmer, uncovered, about 8 minutes or until apple is tender. Drain; gently cut each apple in half lengthways. Refrigerate 20 minutes.

2 Meanwhile, place ingredients for sweet mustard dressing in screw-top jar; shake well.

3 Remove excess fat from duck; rub duck with combined salt, pepper and ginger. Prick duck skins with fork several times. Cook duck, skin-side down, in heated oiled large frying pan about 8 minutes or until crisp. Turn duck; cook about 5 minutes or until cooked as desired. Cover duck; stand 5 minutes, then slice thinly.

4 Meanwhile, heat butter in medium frying pan; cook apple, turning occasionally, until caramelised.

5 Combine spinach and onion in medium bowl; divide among serving plates. Top with duck, apple and nuts, drizzle with dressing.

prep & cook time *45 minutes (+ refrigeration)* serves *4*
nutritional count per serving *72.6g total fat (23g saturated fat); 3290kJ (787 cal); 12.6g carbohydrate; 21.5g protein; 2.7g fibre*

barbecued duck & lychee salad

1kg chinese barbecued duck
565g can lychees in syrup, drained, halved
6 trimmed red radishes (90g), sliced thinly
60g mizuna, torn
½ cup coarsely chopped fresh mint leaves
2 green onions, sliced thinly

kaffir lime and chilli dressing
¼ cup (60m) lime juice
1 tablespoon olive oil
1 teaspoon fish sauce
1 teaspoon grated palm sugar
2 fresh kaffir lime leaves, sliced thinly
1 fresh small red thai chilli, chopped finely
1 clove garlic, crushed

1 Remove skin and meat from duck; discard bones. Slice skin thickly and meat thinly.

2 Place ingredients for kaffir lime and chilli dressing in screw-top jar; shake well.

3 Place duck and dressing in large bowl with remaining ingredients; toss gently to combine.

prep time *25 minutes* serves *4*
nutritional count per serving *41.9g total fat (11.8g saturated fat); 2416kJ (578 cal); 20.3g carbohydrate; 29.6g protein; 2.7g fibre*

turkey, cranberry & peanut salad

1.5kg boneless turkey breast
1.5 litres (6 cups) water
½ cup (125ml) red wine vinegar
1 teaspoon dijon mustard
¼ cup (60ml) light olive oil
⅔ cup (90g) dried cranberries
3 trimmed celery stalks (300g), sliced thinly
1¼ cups (100g) bean sprouts
1 cup (50g) snow pea sprouts
½ cup (70g) roasted unsalted peanuts
½ cup firmly packed fresh mint leaves, torn
1 butter lettuce, leaves separated

1 Cut turkey into three equal-sized pieces. Bring the water to the boil in large saucepan; add turkey. Simmer, covered, about 35 minutes or until turkey is cooked. Cool turkey in poaching liquid 15 minutes. Drain turkey; shred coarsely.

2 Combine vinegar, mustard and oil in large bowl. Add turkey, cranberries, celery, sprouts, nuts and mint; toss gently to combine. Serve salad with lettuce leaves.

prep & cook time *1 hour 10 minutes (+ cooling)* serves *6*
nutritional count per serving *23.1g total fat (4.1g saturated fat); 2019kJ (483 cal); 6.7g carbohydrate; 59.7g protein; 4.2g fibre*

barbecued duck & lychee salad

turkey, cranberry & peanut salad

chicken caesar salad

4 slices white bread (180g)
2 tablespoons olive oil
4 rindless bacon rashers (260g), sliced thinly
3 cups (480g) coarsely chopped barbecued chicken
1 large cos lettuce, trimmed, torn
6 green onions, sliced thinly
1 cup (80g) flaked parmesan cheese

caesar dressing
¾ cup (225g) whole-egg mayonnaise
1 tablespoon lemon juice
4 drained anchovy fillets, chopped finely
3 teaspoons dijon mustard
1 tablespoon water

1 Preheat oven to 180°C/160°C fan-forced.

2 Make caesar dressing.

3 Remove crusts from bread; discard crusts, cut bread into 2cm squares; toss with oil in medium bowl. Place bread, in single layer, on oven tray; toast in oven, 10 minutes.

4 Cook bacon in small frying pan, stirring, until browned and crisp. Drain on absorbent paper.

5 Combine half of the chicken, half of the bacon, half of the croûtons and half of the dressing in large bowl with lettuce, half of the onion and half of the cheese; toss to combine.

6 Divide salad among serving plates. Top with remaining chicken, bacon, croûtons, onion and cheese; drizzle with remaining dressing.

caesar dressing Blend or process ingredients until mixture is smooth.

prep & cook time *25 minutes* serves *4*
nutritional count per serving *49.9g total fat (12.3g saturated fat); 3390kJ (811 cal); 35.6g carbohydrate; 52.6g protein; 6.3g fibre*

smoked chicken & spinach salad

duck & mango salad

smoked chicken & spinach salad

350g smoked chicken breast fillets, sliced thinly
3 trimmed celery stalks (300g), sliced thinly
3 small tomatoes (270g), quartered, seeded
100g baby spinach leaves
4 hard-boiled eggs, quartered
2 green onions, sliced thinly
½ cup (70g) slivered almonds, roasted

cumin mayonnaise
2 teaspoons cumin seeds, toasted
½ cup (150g) mayonnaise
¼ cup (60ml) lemon juice

1 Make cumin mayonnaise.

2 Place chicken, celery, tomato, spinach, egg, onion and nuts in large bowl; toss gently to combine.

3 Divide salad among serving plates; drizzle with mayonnaise.

cumin mayonnaise Using mortar and pestle, crush seeds finely; combine with mayonnaise and juice in small bowl.

prep & cook time *30 minutes* serves *4*
nutritional count per serving *33.5g total fat (5.3g saturated fat); 2044kJ (489 cal); 11.3g carbohydrate; 34g protein; 4.7g fibre*

duck & mango salad

¼ cup (60ml) lime juice
1 tablespoon sweet chilli sauce
1kg chinese barbecued duck
2 teaspoons peanut oil
500g silver beet, trimmed, chopped coarsely
1 cup loosely packed fresh coriander leaves
3 cups (240g) bean sprouts
1 medium mango (430g), sliced thinly
2 limes, cut into wedges

1 Combine juice and sauce in small jug.

2 Remove skin then meat from duck; discard bones, slice skin thinly.

3 Heat oil in wok; stir-fry skin until crisp. Drain. Slice duck meat thinly; stir-fry until hot.

4 Place silver beet, coriander, sprouts, mango, duck and juice mixture in large bowl; toss gently to combine. Sprinkle salad with slivered duck skin, serve with lime wedges.

prep & cook time *30 minutes* serves *4*
nutritional count per serving *39.8g total fat (11.6g saturated fat); 2261kJ (541 cal); 12.5g carbohydrate; 31.8g protein; 4.7g fibre*

meat salads

269

grilled veal & radicchio salad, page 272

In summer, much the nicest way to eat meat is in a salad. It can be cooked in advance, rested (to make it tender) and eaten warm or cold, so your kitchen doesn't get too hot just before you serve lunch or dinner.

271

grilled veal & radicchio salad

600g veal fillet
1 tablespoon olive oil
1 clove garlic, crushed
1 teaspoon finely grated lemon rind
½ teaspoon sweet paprika
2 medium radicchio (400g), trimmed, quartered
250g red grape tomatoes, halved
1 medium yellow capsicum (200g), chopped coarsely
1 small red onion (100g), sliced thinly

paprika mayonnaise
½ cup (150g) mayonnaise
1 tablespoon lemon juice
1 teaspoon sweet paprika

1   Combine veal, oil, garlic, rind and paprika in medium bowl; refrigerate 3 hours or overnight.

2   Combine ingredients for paprika mayonnaise in small bowl.

3   Cook veal on heated oiled grill plate (or grill or barbecue) until cooked as desired. Cover veal; stand 5 minutes, then slice thinly.

4   Meanwhile, cook radicchio on heated oiled grill plate until heated through.

5   Combine veal and remaining ingredients in medium bowl.

6   Divide radicchio among serving plates; top with veal mixture, drizzle with mayonnaise.

prep & cook time *20 minutes (+ refrigeration)* serves *4*
nutritional count per serving *19.4g total fat (2.6g saturated fat); 1584kJ (379 cal); 12.7g carbohydrate; 36.5g protein; 4.1g fibre*

spicy pork & apple salad

350g pork fillet
2 tablespoons lime juice
1 tablespoon finely chopped fresh oregano
2 cloves garlic, crushed
1 teaspoon ground cumin
cooking-oil spray
200g watercress, trimmed
2 medium apples (300g), sliced thickly
250g red grape tomatoes, halved
2 tablespoons finely chopped fresh mint

1   Combine pork, juice, oregano, garlic and cumin in medium bowl.

2   Spray heated medium frying pan with cooking-oil spray for 1 second; cook pork until browned all over and cooked through. Cover; stand 10 minutes then slice pork thinly.

3   Place pork in large bowl with watercress, apple, tomatoes and mint. Serve with lime wedges, if you like.

prep & cook time *15 minutes* serves *4*
nutritional count per serving *2.6g total fat (0.7g saturated fat); 631kJ (151 cal); 9.4g carbohydrate; 20.6g protein; 3.6g fibre*

spicy pork & apple salad

peppered lamb with watercress

2 tablespoons mixed peppercorns
1 tablespoon olive oil
600g lamb fillets
1 cup (160g) fresh or frozen peas
250g yellow teardrop tomatoes, halved
100g watercress, trimmed
200g fetta cheese, cut into thin strips
¼ cup coarsely chopped fresh mint

white wine vinaigrette
¼ cup (60ml) white wine vinegar
1 tablespoon olive oil
1 clove garlic, crushed

1 Using mortar and pestle, crush peppercorns until ground coarsely. Combine ground peppercorns, oil and lamb in medium bowl.

2 Cook lamb in heated oiled large frying pan until cooked as desired. Cover lamb; stand 5 minutes, then slice thinly.

3 Meanwhile, place ingredients for white wine vinaigrette in screw-top jar; shake well.

4 Boil, steam or microwave peas until tender; drain. Rinse under cold water; drain.

5 Place lamb, peas and vinaigrette in large bowl with remaining ingredients; toss gently to combine.

prep & cook time *30 minutes* serves *4*
nutritional count per serving *31.1g total fat (12g saturated fat); 2006kJ (480 cal); 5.1g carbohydrate; 43.2g protein; 5g fibre*

lamb & beetroot salad

800g lamb fillets
1 tablespoon honey
1 tablespoon balsamic vinegar
1 clove garlic, crushed
500g baby beetroot
2 teaspoons olive oil
1 lebanese cucumber (130g), seeded, sliced thinly
200g ricotta cheese, crumbled

honey balsamic dressing
¼ cup (60ml) olive oil
2 tablespoons balsamic vinegar
1 tablespoon honey
1 teaspoon dijon mustard

1 Combine lamb, honey, vinegar and garlic in medium bowl; cover, refrigerate 3 hours or overnight.

2 Preheat oven to 220°C/200°C fan-forced.

3 Remove unblemished leaves from the beetroot, reserve for later use. Peel and quarter beetroot. Place on oven tray; drizzle with oil. Roast, uncovered, about 30 minutes or until tender.

4 Meanwhile, cook lamb in heated oiled large frying pan until cooked as desired. Cover lamb; stand 5 minutes, then slice thinly.

5 Combine ingredients for honey balsamic dressing in small bowl.

6 Place lamb, beetroot and dressing in large bowl with beetroot leaves and cucumber; toss gently to combine. Serve salad, sprinkled with cheese.

prep & cook time *40 minutes (+ refrigeration)* serves *4*
nutritional count per serving *28.9g total fat (9.1g saturated fat); 2228kJ (533 cal); 19.2g carbohydrate; 47.9g protein; 2.8g fibre*

peppered lamb with watercress

lamb & beetroot salad

lamb, spinach & spiced peach salad

20g butter
1 teaspoon ground coriander
½ teaspoon ground cardamom
¼ teaspoon ground cinnamon
3 medium peaches (450g), peeled, sliced thickly
2 tablespoons brown sugar
1 tablespoon raspberry vinegar
800g lamb backstrap
1 large red onion (300g), sliced thinly
150g snow peas, trimmed, sliced thinly
150g baby spinach leaves
2 fresh long red chillies, sliced thinly

raspberry dressing
120g raspberries
2 tablespoons raspberry vinegar
2 tablespoons olive oil
1 teaspoon sugar
1 teaspoon dijon mustard

1   Melt butter in large frying pan; cook spices, stirring, until fragrant. Add peach; cook, stirring, about 2 minutes or until just tender. Add sugar and vinegar; cook, stirring, until sugar dissolves. Remove peach from pan with slotted spoon; place in large bowl.

2   Add lamb to sugar mixture in pan; cook, uncovered, over low heat until browned both sides and cooked as desired. Cover lamb; stand 10 minutes then slice thickly.

3   Meanwhile, make raspberry dressing.

4   Add lamb and remaining ingredients to bowl of peaches; toss gently to combine. Serve salad drizzled with dressing.

raspberry dressing Blend or process ingredients until mixture is smooth.

prep & cook time *35 minutes*   serves *4*
nutritional count per serving *31.3g total fat (12g saturated fat); 2303kJ (551 cal); 21.3g carbohydrate; 46g protein; 5.6g fibre*

blackened steak salad

2 pocket pitta breads (170g)
500g beef fillet
2 teaspoons hot paprika
1 teaspoon ground black pepper
½ teaspoon cayenne pepper
¼ teaspoon dried oregano
¼ teaspoon dried thyme
3 medium tomatoes (450g), chopped finely
1 large green capsicum (350g), chopped finely
1 lebanese cucumber (130g), seeded, chopped finely
½ cup coarsely chopped fresh mint
1 tablespoon olive oil
1 tablespoon balsamic vinegar
1 clove garlic, crushed

1   Preheat grill to hot.

2   Split breads in half; grill both sides until browned lightly. Break into coarse pieces.

3   Rub beef with combined spices; cook on heated oiled grill plate (or grill or barbecue) until cooked as desired. Cover beef; stand 5 minutes, then slice thinly.

4   Meanwhile, combine remaining ingredients in large bowl. Arrange beef on serving plates; top with salad. Serve with bread.

prep & cook time *30 minutes*   serves *4*
nutritional count per serving   *13.3g total fat (3.9g saturated fat); 1542kJ (369 cal); 26.8g carbohydrate; 32.9g protein; 4.1g fibre*

lamb with eggplant & tomato salad

1 large eggplant (500g)
cooking-oil spray
1 medium red onion (170g), sliced thickly
2 tablespoons red wine vinegar
1 tablespoon brown sugar
4 cloves garlic
50g butter, chopped
¼ cup (60ml) olive oil
1 tablespoon finely chopped fresh flat-leaf parsley
500g baby truss tomatoes
400g lamb backstraps
3 teaspoons sumac
80g baby rocket leaves
⅓ cup (55g) sultanas

1   Preheat oven to 220°C/200°C fan-forced.

2   Cut eggplant into four 1cm slices; coat with cooking-oil spray. Cook on heated grill plate (or grill or barbecue) until tender.

3   Combine onion, vinegar, sugar, garlic, butter and 2 tablespoons of the oil in large shallow baking dish. Roast, in oven, stirring once, 10 minutes. Remove from oven, stir in parsley; cool 5 minutes.

4   Meanwhile, place tomatoes on oven tray; drizzle with remaining oil. Roast 10 minutes.

5   Rub lamb with sumac; cook on heated oiled grill plate (or grill or barbecue) until cooked as desired. Cover lamb; stand 5 minutes, then slice thickly.

6   Place rocket, sultanas and onion mixture in large bowl; toss gently to combine. Divide eggplant among serving plates; top with rocket mixture, lamb and tomatoes.

prep & cook time *45 minutes*   serves *4*
nutritional count per serving   *30.3g total fat (10.4g saturated fat); 1969kJ (471 cal); 22.6g carbohydrate; 24.3g protein; 6.9g fibre*

blackened steak salad

lamb with eggplant & tomato salad

beef & beetroot with horseradish crème fraîche

500g piece beef eye fillet, trimmed
2 tablespoons wholegrain mustard
1 tablespoon horseradish cream
2 tablespoons olive oil
1kg baby beetroot, trimmed
150g baby rocket leaves
2 lebanese cucumbers (260g), sliced thinly
1 cup loosely packed fresh flat-leaf parsley leaves

parmesan croûtons
1 small french bread stick (150g)
1 tablespoon olive oil
½ cup (40g) finely grated parmesan cheese

horseradish crème fraîche
¼ cup (60g) crème fraîche
2 tablespoons horseradish cream
1 tablespoon lemon juice

1 Preheat oven to 220°C/200°C fan-forced.

2 Tie beef with kitchen string at 3cm intervals. Combine mustard, horseradish and oil in small jug; brush beef all over with mixture.

3 Place beef in medium oiled baking dish with beetroot; roast, uncovered, 10 minutes.

4 Reduce heat to 200°C/180°C fan-forced; roast about 20 minutes or until beef and beetroot are cooked. Cover beef; stand 15 minutes then slice thinly. Peel and halve beetroot.

5 Make parmesan croûtons and horseradish crème fraîche.

6 Place rocket, cucumber, parsley and beetroot in large bowl; toss gently to combine. Serve salad topped with croûtons and beef, drizzled with crème fraîche.

parmesan croûtons Slice bread thinly; brush slices with oil, place on oven tray. Brown, in oven, towards end of beef cooking time; sprinkle with cheese, return to oven until cheese melts.

horseradish crème fraîche Combine ingredients in small bowl.

prep & cook time *45 minutes (+ standing)* serves 4
nutritional count per serving *33.8g total fat (12.2g saturated fat); 2704kJ (647 cal); 40.7g carbohydrate; 40.2g protein; 10.5g fibre*

pork & apple salad

600g pork fillet
2 tablespoons brown sugar
2 teaspoons wholegrain mustard
2 teaspoons finely grated orange rind
1 tablespoon olive oil
10g butter
1 medium green-skinned apple (150g), unpeeled,
    halved, cut into 5mm-thick slices
60g baby spinach leaves

spiced orange dressing
¼ cup (60ml) olive oil
2 tablespoons orange juice
1 tablespoon cider vinegar
1 teaspoon mixed spice

1   Combine pork, sugar, mustard and rind in
medium bowl.

2   Heat oil in medium frying pan; cook pork until
cooked as desired. Cover pork; stand 5 minutes
then slice thinly.

3   Melt butter in same frying pan; cook apple until
caramelised.

4   Meanwhile, place ingredients for spiced orange
dressing in screw-top jar; shake well.

5   Place apple mixture, dressing and spinach in medium
bowl; toss gently to combine. Arrange pork among
serving plates; top with apple salad. Drizzle with any
remaining dressing from bowl.

prep & cook time *30 minutes* serves *4*
nutritional count per serving *23.8g total fat (5.1g
saturated fat); 1639kJ (392 cal); 10.6g carbohydrate;
33.5g protein; 1.1g fibre*

chorizo & capsicum salad

2 large red capsicums (700g)
2 chorizo sausages (340g), sliced thinly
280g jar artichoke hearts in brine, drained, halved
200g red grape tomatoes, halved
80g curly endive leaves
½ cup firmly packed fresh flat-leaf parsley leaves

herb and garlic dressing
2 tablespoons olive oil
2 tablespoons white wine vinegar
1 tablespoon lemon juice
1 tablespoon finely chopped fresh basil
1 tablespoon finely chopped fresh oregano
2 cloves garlic, chopped finely

1   Quarter capsicums; discard seeds and membranes. Roast
capsicum under hot grill, skin-side up, until skin blisters and
blackens. Cover capsicum pieces with plastic or paper for
5 minutes; peel away skin then cut pieces in half diagonally.

2   Meanwhile, cook chorizo in large frying pan, stirring
occasionally, until browned. Drain on absorbent paper.

3   Combine ingredients for herb and garlic dressing in
small bowl.

4   Place capsicum, chorizo and dressing in large bowl
with remaining ingredients; toss gently to combine.

prep & cook time *25 minutes* serves *4*
nutritional count per serving *36g total fat (10.8g saturated
fat); 1885kJ (451 cal); 16.4g carbohydrate; 20.5g protein;
3.9g fibre*

pork & apple salad

chorizo & capsicum salad

crisp pork belly with wombok salad

2 cups (500ml) salt-reduced chicken stock
⅓ cup (80ml) chinese cooking wine
½ cup (125ml) lime juice
¼ cup (60ml) japanese soy sauce
2 dried red chillies
2 star anise
1 tablespoon coarsely chopped fresh
    coriander root and stem mixture
2cm piece fresh ginger (10g), sliced thinly
2 cloves garlic, halved
2 fresh kaffir lime leaves, torn
800g piece pork belly
¼ cup (60ml) oyster sauce
⅓ cup (90g) firmly packed grated palm sugar
2 tablespoons fish sauce
1 tablespoon peanut oil
2 fresh long red chillies, chopped finely
2cm piece fresh ginger (10g), grated
1 clove garlic, crushed
½ medium wombok (500g), shredded finely
1 medium red capsicum (200g), sliced thinly
1 large carrot (180g), sliced thinly
1 cup (80g) bean sprouts
2 green onions, sliced thinly
½ cup loosely packed fresh coriander leaves
½ cup loosely packed vietnamese mint leaves
½ cup (70g) roasted unsalted peanuts,
    chopped coarsely
¼ cup (20g) fried shallots

1 Combine stock, wine, half the juice, soy sauce, dried chillies, star anise, coriander root and stem mixture, sliced ginger, halved garlic, lime leaves and pork in large deep flameproof dish; bring to the boil. Reduce heat; simmer, covered tightly, about 1½ hours or until pork is tender.

2 Remove pork from dish. Strain broth through muslin-lined sieve into medium saucepan; discard solids. Bring broth to the boil; boil, uncovered, 10 minutes.

3 Slice pork lengthways into 1cm-thick slices. Combine pork with half the broth and oyster sauce in large bowl. Cover; refrigerate 2 hours.

4 Meanwhile, to make dressing, stir sugar into remaining broth; bring to the boil, stirring until sugar dissolves. Reduce heat; simmer, uncovered, about 5 minutes or until thickened slightly. Remove from heat; stir in remaining juice, fish sauce, oil, fresh chilli, grated ginger and crushed garlic. Cool dressing.

5 Preheat oven to 240°C/220°C fan-forced. Oil two oven trays, line with baking paper.

6 Drain pork; discard marinade. Place pork, in single layer, on trays; cook, uncovered, turning occasionally, about 20 minutes or until crisp. Cut pork slices into 2cm pieces.

7 Meanwhile, place wombok, capsicum, carrot, sprouts, onion, coriander leaves, mint, nuts and dressing in large bowl; add pork, toss gently to combine.

8 Divide salad among serving bowls, sprinkle with shallots.

prep & cook time *2 hours 45 minutes (+ refrigeration)*
serves *6*
nutritional count per serving *58.7g total fat (17.6g saturated fat); 4009kJ (959 cal); 37.7g carbohydrate; 64.8g protein; 16.8g fibre*

lamb & pasta niçoise

375g penne pasta
¼ cup (60ml) olive oil
600g lamb fillets
4 large tomatoes (880g), chopped coarsely
2 cloves garlic, crushed
1 fresh long red chilli, chopped finely
1 cup (120g) seeded black olives, chopped coarsely
2 tablespoons drained baby capers, rinsed
12 (150g) drained marinated artichoke hearts, quartered
1 cup loosely packed fresh flat-leaf parsley leaves

1 Cook pasta in large saucepan of boiling water, uncovered, until just tender; drain.

2 Meanwhile, heat 1 tablespoon of the oil in large frying pan; cook lamb, in batches, until browned all over and cooked as desired. Stand, covered, 5 minutes; slice thinly.

3 Heat remaining oil in large saucepan; cook tomato, garlic and chilli, stirring, until tomato softens. Stir in olives, capers and artichoke.

4 Return lamb to pan with pasta and parsley; toss gently until heated through.

prep & cook time *30 minutes* serves *4*
nutritional count per serving *29.4g total fat (8.4g saturated fat); 3219kJ (770 cal); 76.3g carbohydrate; 45.4g protein; 7.2g fibre*

cajun-spiced beef salad

750g piece beef fillet
1 tablespoon cajun spice mix
420g can mixed beans, rinsed, drained
2 lebanese cucumbers (260g), halved lengthways, sliced thinly
4 small tomatoes (360g), cut into wedges
1 medium red onion (170g), sliced thinly
1 medium avocado (250g), sliced thickly
½ cup finely chopped fresh coriander

garlic vinaigrette
¼ cup (60ml) lemon juice
¼ cup (60ml) olive oil
2 cloves garlic, crushed

1 Combine ingredients for garlic vinaigrette in small bowl.

2 Sprinkle beef both sides with spice mix; cook on heated oiled grill plate (or grill or barbecue). Cover; stand 5 minutes then slice thinly.

3 Place remaining ingredients in large bowl with dressing; toss gently to combine.

4 Serve salad topped with beef.

prep & cook time *25 minutes* serves *4*
nutritional count per serving *35.3g total fat (8.8g saturated fat); 2445kJ (585 cal); 16.3g carbohydrate; 47.5g protein; 7.5 g fibre*

Cajun spice mix, a blend of ground herbs and spices that can include basil, paprika, tarragon, fennel, thyme or cayenne, is available at most supermarkets and speciality spice shops.

lamb & pasta niçoise

cajun-spiced beef salad

glazed pork & watercress salad

pork & lychee salad

glazed pork & watercress salad

¼ cup (90g) honey
¼ cup (85g) tamarind concentrate
3cm piece fresh ginger (15g), grated
2 cloves garlic, crushed
800g pork fillets
100g watercress, trimmed
1 medium red onion (170g), sliced thinly
2 lebanese cucumbers (260g), seeded, sliced thinly
1 medium yellow capsicum (200g), sliced thinly
½ cup (75g) roasted unsalted cashews

1 Combine honey, tamarind, ginger and garlic in small jug. Combine pork and a third of the honey mixture in medium bowl.

2 Cook pork on heated oiled grill plate (or grill or barbecue) until browned all over and cooked as desired. Cover; stand 10 minutes then slice thickly.

3 Meanwhile, place remaining ingredients in medium bowl with half the remaining honey mixture; toss gently to combine.

4 Drizzle pork with remaining honey mixture; serve with salad.

prep & cook time *30 minutes* serves *4*
nutritional count per serving *14.1g total fat (3.2g saturated fat); 1885kJ (451 cal); 29.9g carbohydrate; 49.6g protein; 4.3g fibre*

pork & lychee salad

1 tablespoon peanut oil
300g pork fillet
565g can lychees, rinsed, drained, halved
1 medium red capsicum (200g), sliced thinly
10cm stick fresh lemon grass (20g), sliced thinly
2 fresh kaffir lime leaves, shredded finely
100g watercress
2 tablespoons coarsely chopped fresh vietnamese mint
2 tablespoons drained thinly sliced pickled ginger
2 tablespoons fried shallot

pickled garlic dressing
1 tablespoon drained finely chopped pickled garlic
2 fresh small red thai chillies, seeded, sliced thinly
1 tablespoon rice vinegar
1 tablespoon lime juice
1 tablespoon fish sauce
1 tablespoon palm sugar

1 Combine ingredients for pickled garlic dressing in small bowl.

2 Heat oil in wok; cook pork, turning, until browned all over and cooked as desired. Cover, stand 10 minutes; slice thinly. Place pork in medium bowl with dressing; toss to coat pork all over. Stand 10 minutes.

3 Meanwhile, place lychees, capsicum, lemon grass, lime leaves, watercress and mint in large bowl; toss gently to combine.

4 Add pork mixture to lychee mixture; toss gently to combine. Serve sprinkled with pickled ginger and fried shallot.

prep & cook time *30 minutes* serves *4*
nutritional count per serving *6.9g total fat (1.5g saturated fat); 911kJ (218 cal); 18.1g carbohydrate; 19.1g protein; 3.3g fibre*

Gypsy ham is identified by the fact that it is twice hickory smoked after the rind has been removed. If gypsy ham is not available from your local delicatessen, use double-smoked ham instead.

gypsy ham salad with mustard vinaigrette

300g snow peas, trimmed
2 medium avocados (500g), cut into cubes
1⅓ cups (200g) drained semi-dried tomatoes, chopped coarsely
150g baby spinach leaves
350g gypsy ham, torn into large pieces

mustard vinaigrette
2 cloves garlic, crushed
2 tablespoons white wine vinegar
2 tablespoons finely chopped fresh flat-leaf parsley
1cm piece fresh ginger (5g), grated
1 tablespoon wholegrain mustard
1 tablespoon warm water
¼ cup (60ml) extra light olive oil

1 Boil, steam or microwave snow peas until tender; drain. Rinse under cold water; drain.

2 Meanwhile, place ingredients for mustard vinaigrette in screw-top jar; shake well.

3 Place snow peas in large bowl with remaining ingredients; toss gently to combine. Divide salad among serving plates; drizzle with vinaigrette.

prep & cook time *25 minutes* serves *4*
nutritional count per serving *40.9g total fat (7.8g saturated fat); 2429kJ (581 cal); 21.5g carbohydrate; 27g protein; 11.7g fibre*

pancetta & mushroom salad

lamb & fetta salad

pancetta & mushroom salad

200g swiss brown mushrooms, quartered
¼ cup (60ml) balsamic vinegar
8 slices pancetta (120g)
100g baby spinach leaves, trimmed
2 tablespoons drained baby capers, rinsed
2 green onions, chopped finely
1 tablespoon olive oil
1 clove garlic, crushed

1 Combine mushrooms with 2 tablespoons of the vinegar in small bowl.

2 Cook pancetta in medium oiled frying pan until crisp; chop coarsely.

3 Drain mushrooms; discard vinegar. Cook mushrooms in same pan until tender.

4 Place pancetta, mushrooms and remaining vinegar in large large bowl with remaining ingredients; toss gently to combine.

prep & cook time *20 minutes* serves *6*
nutritional count per serving *6g total fat (1.5g saturated fat); 360kJ (86 cal); 1.3g carbohydrate; 5.6g protein; 1.6g fibre*

lamb & fetta salad

1 tablespoon vegetable oil
600g lamb fillets
200g fetta cheese, crumbled
250g witlof, trimmed, leaves separated
150g baby spinach leaves, trimmed

warm walnut dressing
2 cloves garlic, crushed
1 teaspoon finely grated lemon rind
¼ cup (60ml) olive oil
2 tablespoons cider vinegar
½ cup (55g) coarsely chopped roasted walnuts

1 Heat oil in large frying pan; cook lamb, uncovered, about 10 minutes. Cover; stand 5 minutes then slice thickly.

2 Make warm walnut dressing.

3 Place lamb in medium bowl with cheese, witlof and spinach; toss gently to combine. Serve salad drizzled with dressing.

warm walnut dressing Cook garlic, rind, oil and vinegar in small pan, stirring, until hot. Remove from heat; stir in nuts.

prep & cook time *25 minutes* serves *4*
nutritional count per serving *52.8g total fat (16.8g saturated fat); 2742kJ (656 cal); 1.2g carbohydrate; 43.8g protein; 3.2g fibre*

fruit salads

strawberries romanoff, page 298

The salads in this chapter are a mixture of starters, accompaniments and desserts. Some, such as the watermelon with chilli herbed salad can be eaten anytime – serve it chilled for best results.

strawberries romanoff

500g strawberries, halved
1½ tablespoons orange-flavoured liqueur
2 teaspoons icing sugar
2 tablespoons icing sugar, extra
½ cup (125ml) thickened cream

1 Combine strawberries, liqueur and icing sugar in large bowl; refrigerate 30 minutes. Drain strawberries over small bowl; reserve liquid. Divide three-quarters of the strawberries among serving dishes.

2 Blend or process remaining strawberries, extra icing sugar and reserved liquid until smooth. Beat cream in small bowl with electric mixer until soft peaks form; fold in strawberry mixture.

3 Top strawberries with strawberry cream.

prep time *15 minutes (+ refrigeration)* serves *4*
nutritional count per serving *11.8g total fat (7.6g saturated fat); 790kJ (189 cal); 14.2g carbohydrate; 2.8g protein; 2.8g fibre*

vanilla & lime asian fruit salad

1 litre (4 cups) water
1 cup (270g) grated palm sugar
1 vanilla bean
2cm piece fresh ginger (10g), chopped finely
3 star anise
1 tablespoon finely grated lime rind
⅓ cup (80ml) lime juice
½ cup coarsely chopped fresh vietnamese mint
2 large mangoes (1.2kg), chopped coarsely
3 star fruit (450g), sliced thinly
2 large oranges (600g), segmented
1 large pineapple (2kg), chopped coarsely
1 medium papaya (1kg), chopped coarsely
½ cup (125ml) passionfruit pulp
12 rambutans (500g), halved
12 lychees (300g), halved

1 Stir the water and sugar in medium saucepan over high heat until sugar dissolves; bring to the boil. Reduce heat; simmer without stirring, uncovered, 5 minutes. Split vanilla bean in half lengthways; scrape seeds into pan. Add pod, ginger and star anise; simmer, uncovered, about 10 minutes or until syrup thickens. Discard pod; cool to room temperature. Stir in rind, juice and mint.

2 Combine remaining ingredients in large bowl. Pour syrup over fruit; stir gently to combine. Refrigerate fruit salad, covered, until cold.

prep & cook time *35 minutes (+ cooling & refrigeration)* serves *8*
nutritional count per serving *0.9g total fat (0g saturated fat); 1626kJ (389 cal); 82.8g carbohydrate; 5.2g protein; 12.4g fibre*

vanilla & lime asian fruit salad

citrus salad with granita

2 medium oranges (480g)
2 small pink grapefruits (700g)
⅓ cup finely chopped fresh mint
2 tablespoons icing sugar
1 tablespoon lime juice
2 cups ice cubes

1 Segment orange and grapefruit into medium bowl.

2 Blend or process mint, sugar, juice and ice until ice is crushed; serve with fruit.

prep time *15 minutes* serves *4*
nutritional count per serving *0.4g total fat (0g saturated fat); 385kJ (92 cal); 18.1g carbohydrate; 2.1g protein; 2.7g fibre*

endive, lychee & papaya salad

3 witlof (375g)
1 small papaya (650g), chopped coarsely
½ cup loosely packed fresh mint leaves
½ cup loosely packed fresh thai basil leaves
2 fresh long red chillies, sliced thinly
150g curly endive
565g can lychees, drained

passionfruit dressing
⅓ cup (80ml) passionfruit pulp
¼ cup (60ml) lemon juice
¼ cup (60ml) light olive oil

1 Cut bases from witlof; slice leaves thickly lengthways.

2 Place ingredients for passionfruit dressing in screw-top jar; shake well.

3 Place witlof in large bowl with remaining ingredients and dressing; toss gently to combine.

prep time *15 minutes* serves *8*
nutritional count per serving *7.2g total fat (1g saturated fat); 573kJ (137 cal); 13.9g carbohydrate; 1.9g protein; 5g fibre*

citrus salad with granita

endive, lychee & papaya salad

orange & radish salad

pear, walnut & fetta salad

orange & radish salad

10 trimmed medium red radishes (150g), sliced thinly
4 large oranges (1.2kg), segmented
1 small red onion (100g), sliced thinly
2 tablespoons coarsely chopped fresh flat-leaf parsley
2 tablespoons coarsely chopped fresh coriander
¼ cup (60ml) orange juice

1 Assemble radish, orange and onion on serving platter; sprinkle with parsley and coriander, drizzle with juice.

2 Cover salad; refrigerate 1 hour before serving.

prep time *20 minutes (+ refrigeration)* serves *4*
nutritional count per serving *0.3g total fat (0g saturated fat); 447kJ (107 cal); 20.1g carbohydrate; 3g protein; 5.2g fibre*

pear, walnut & fetta salad

1 butter lettuce
1 medium pear (230g), cored
⅓ cup (35g) roasted walnuts, chopped coarsely
40g snow pea sprouts, trimmed
50g fetta cheese, crumbled
35g shaved parmesan cheese

walnut dressing
1 tablespoon walnut oil
2 teaspoons wholegrain mustard
2 tablespoons white wine vinegar
1 tablespoon finely chopped fresh chives

1 Place ingredients for walnut dressing in screw-top jar; shake well.

2 Separate lettuce leaves; tear leaves roughly.

3 Slice unpeeled pear into thin wedges.

4 Place lettuce, pear and dressing in large bowl with remaining ingredients; toss gently to combine.

prep time *20 minutes* serves *4*
nutritional count per serving *16.6g total fat (5g saturated fat); 957kJ (229 cal); 10.4g carbohydrate; 8.4g protein; 3.3g fibre*

tropical fruit salad

1 cup (250ml) water
2 tablespoons elderflower cordial
1 tablespoon caster sugar
1 vanilla bean, split lengthways
½ medium rockmelon (850g), chopped coarsely
½ small papaya (325g), sliced thinly
3 medium kiwifruit (255g), halved, sliced thinly
1 large banana (230g), sliced thinly

1 Combine the water, cordial and sugar in small saucepan. Scrape vanilla seeds into pan then add pod, stir over medium heat until sugar dissolves; bring to the boil. Reduce heat; simmer, uncovered, about 10 minutes or until syrup thickens slightly. Transfer syrup to medium heatproof jug. Cover; refrigerate 1 hour.

2 Combine fruit in large bowl. Pour syrup mixture over fruit.

prep & cook time *20 minutes (+ refrigeration)*   serves *4*
nutritional count per serving *0.4g total fat (0g saturated fat); 644kJ (154 cal); 32.1g carbohydrate; 2.4g protein; 5.4g fibre*

Elderflower cordial is available from most supermarkets. You can substitute elderflower cordial with orange, lemon or lime cordial.

green papaya salad

100g bean thread noodles
1 small green papaya (650g)
150g sugar snap peas, trimmed, halved diagonally
2 fresh long red chillies, sliced thinly
⅓ cup firmly packed fresh mint leaves
250g cherry tomatoes, quartered

palm sugar dressing
⅓ cup (80ml) lime juice
2 tablespoons grated palm sugar
1 tablespoon fish sauce

1 Place noodles in medium heatproof bowl, cover with boiling water; stand until almost tender, drain. Rinse under cold water; drain.

2 Meanwhile, peel papaya; quarter lengthways, discard seeds. Grate papaya coarsely.

3 Place ingredients for palm sugar dressing in screw-top jar; shake well.

4 Place noodles, papaya and dressing in large bowl with peas, chilli, mint and tomato; toss gently to combine.

prep & cook time *20 minutes* serves *6*
nutritional count per serving *0.4g total fat (0g saturated fat); 472kJ (113 cal); 22.5g carbohydrate; 2.7g protein; 3.4g fibre*

roasted pear & spinach salad

4 medium pears (920g), peeled, cored, sliced thickly
2 tablespoons lemon juice
2 tablespoons brown sugar
100g baby spinach leaves
50g baby rocket leaves
¼ cup (20g) flaked parmesan cheese
¼ cup coarsely chopped fresh chives

balsamic mustard dressing
2 tablespoons balsamic vinegar
1 tablespoon wholegrain mustard
1 teaspoon olive oil

1 Preheat oven to 200°C/180°C fan-forced. Line oven tray with baking paper.

2 Combine pears, juice and sugar in large bowl. Place pears, in single layer, on oven tray; roast, uncovered, about 30 minutes, brushing with juices occasionally, or until tender. Cool 20 minutes.

3 Meanwhile, place ingredients for balsamic mustard dressing in screw-top jar; shake well.

4 Place pears and dressing in large bowl with spinach, rocket, cheese and chives; toss gently to combine.

prep & cook time *40 minutes (+ cooling)* serves *4*
nutritional count per serving *3.2g total fat (1.2g saturated fat); 761kJ (182 cal); 32g carbohydrate; 3.7g protein; 4.4g fibre*

green papaya salad

roasted pear & spinach salad

pomegranate salad with chilli popcorn

¼ cup (60ml) vegetable oil
40g butter
¼ cup (60g) popping corn
1 teaspoon dried chilli flakes
¼ teaspoon sea salt flakes
4 medium oranges (1kg)
1 cup (50g) snow pea sprouts
½ cup (125ml) pomegranate pulp
6 red radishes (210g), trimmed, sliced thinly

orange dressing
¼ cup (60ml) olive oil
2 tablespoons orange juice
1 tablespoon white wine vinegar
1 teaspoon honey

1 Heat oil in medium saucepan, add butter, corn and chilli; cook, covered, over high heat, shaking pan vigorously until corn stops popping. Drain on absorbent paper; sprinkle with salt.

2 Place ingredients for orange dressing in screw-top jar; shake well.

3 Peel oranges thickly; cut crossways into 5mm slices.

4 Stack orange slices, sprouts, pomegranate and radish on serving platter; drizzle with dressing, sprinkle over popcorn.

prep and cook time *20 minutes* serves *8*
nutritional count per serving *18.2g total fat (4.6g saturated fat); 1003kJ (240 cal); 14.9g carbohydrate; 2.6g protein; 4.3g fibre*

You need to buy a medium pomegranate (320g) to get ½ cup pulp. To remove the pulp from the pomegranate, cut it in half, then hit the back of the fruit with a wooden spoon – the seeds usually fall out easily. Discard the shell and white pith.

balsamic strawberries

500g strawberries, halved
2 tablespoons icing sugar
1 tablespoon balsamic vinegar
¼ cup loosely packed fresh mint leaves
½ cup (140g) low-fat natural yogurt

1 Combine strawberries, icing sugar and vinegar in medium bowl. Cover; refrigerate 20 minutes.

2 Sprinkle mint over strawberries; serve with yogurt.

prep time *10 minutes (+ refrigeration)* serves *4*
nutritional count per serving *0.2g total fat (0g saturated fat); 293kJ (70 cal); 11g carbohydrate; 4.3g protein; 3g fibre*

strawberries in orange syrup

¼ cup (60ml) water
2 tablespoons grated palm sugar
2 teaspoons finely grated orange rind
2 tablespoons orange juice
500g strawberries, quartered
¼ cup coarsely chopped fresh mint
⅔ cup (160g) crème fraîche

1 Stir sugar in small saucepan, over low heat, until sugar dissolves; bring to the boil. Boil, uncovered, without stirring, about 3 minutes or until syrup thickens slightly. Remove from heat; stir in rind and juice. Cool.

2 Combine strawberries and in medium bowl with syrup; refrigerate 30 minutes.

3 Divide strawberry mixture among bowls; serve with crème fraîche.

prep & cook time *20 minutes (+ cooling & refrigeration)* serves *4*
nutrition count per serving *15.2g total fat (9.9g saturated fat); 840kJ (201 cal); 11.8g carbohydrate; 3.2g protein; 3.1g fibre*

balsamic strawberries

strawberries in orange syrup

tropical fruit with orange glaze

1 teaspoon finely grated orange rind
2 tablespoons orange juice
2 tablespoons brown sugar
1 small pineapple (900g), trimmed, halved, sliced thickly
2 medium bananas (400g), quartered
1 star fruit (160g), sliced thickly
¼ cup loosely packed fresh mint leaves

1 To make orange glaze, stir rind, juice and sugar in small saucepan over low heat until sugar dissolves. Cool.

2 Preheat grill.

3 Place glaze in large bowl with fruit; stir to combine. Spread fruit mixture onto two foil-lined oven trays.

4 Grill fruit about 5 minutes or until browned lightly. Serve fruit sprinkled with mint.

prep & cook time *20 minutes* serves *4*
nutritional count per serving *0.3g total fat (0g saturated fat); 640kJ (153 cal); 32.1g carbohydrate; 2.8g protein; 4.8g fibre*

watermelon, mint & fetta salad

2 teaspoons white sugar
¼ cup (60ml) lime juice
½ cup (100g) crumbled fetta cheese
½ small red onion (50g), sliced thinly
½ cup coarsely chopped fresh mint
850g seedless watermelon, cut into wedges

1 Dissolve sugar in small jug with juice.

2 Combine juice mixture in large bowl with cheese, onion and mint.

3 Arrange watermelon on serving plates; spoon cheese mixture over watermelon.

prep time *10 minutes*   serves *4*
nutritional count per serving *6.2g total fat (3.8g saturated fat); 506kJ (121 cal); 10.1g carbohydrate; 5.4g protein; 1.5g fibre*

watermelon & berry salad

2kg piece seedless watermelon
250g strawberries, halved
125g blueberries
¼ cup loosely packed fresh mint leaves

1 Using melon baller, cut watermelon balls.

2 Combine watermelon in medium bowl with berries and mint.

prep time *10 minutes* serves *4*
nutritional count per serving *0.5g total fat (0g saturated fat); 314kJ (75 cal); 14.1g carbohydrate; 1.9g protein; 3.2g fibre*

watermelon with chilli herbed salad

2 limes
½ seedless watermelon (3kg)
1 fresh long red chilli, chopped finely
½ cup finely chopped fresh coriander
¼ cup baby fresh mint leaves
½ cup baby tat soi

lime dressing
¼ cup (60ml) lime juice
¼ cup (60ml) olive oil

1 Cut thin strips of rind from one lime then cut finely; reserve for lime dressing. Peel remaining lime; segment both limes then chop coarsely.

2 Remove and discard skin and white pith from watermelon; cut watermelon in half, then cut into eight 5cm x 8cm blocks. Cut blocks into six 1cm slices.

3 Make lime dressing.

4 Place lime in medium bowl with chilli, coriander, mint and tat soi in; toss gently to combine.

5 Layer watermelon on large platter; sprinkle over lime and herb mixture, drizzle with dressing.

lime dressing Place juice, oil and reserved rind in screw-top jar; shake well.

prep time *15 minutes* serves *8*
nutritional count per serving *7.4g total fat (1g saturated fat); 514kJ (123 cal); 12.4g carbohydrate; 1g protein; 1.7g fibre*

pineapple & kiwifruit salad

summer fruit salad with minted sugar

pineapple & kiwifruit salad

1½ cups (375ml) water
2 x 5cm strips lemon rind
½ cup (125ml) lemon juice
1 tablespoon caster sugar
¼ cup firmly packed fresh basil leaves
1 small pineapple (900g), quartered, sliced thinly
6 medium kiwifruit (510g), sliced thinly
⅓ cup (80ml) passionfruit pulp
1 tablespoon finely shredded fresh basil

1 Combine the water, rind, juice, sugar and basil leaves in medium frying pan; bring to the boil. Reduce heat; simmer, uncovered, 20 minutes. Strain syrup into medium jug; discard rind and basil. Cool 10 minutes; refrigerate.

2 Just before serving, place syrup in large bowl with remaining ingredients; stir to combine.

prep & cook time *40 minutes (+ refrigeration)* serves *4*
nutrition count per serving *0.5g total fat (0g saturated fat); 627kJ (150 cal); 26.6g carbohydrate; 3.6g protein; 9g fibre*

summer fruit salad with minted sugar

¼ cup loosely packed fresh mint leaves
2 tablespoons white sugar
2 teaspoons finely grated lemon rind
2 medium pears (460g), cored, sliced thinly
150g blackberries
125g strawberries, halved
100g seedless green grapes, halved

1 Blend or process mint, sugar and rind until chopped finely.

2 Combine fruit in medium bowl. Serve fruit salad with minted sugar.

prep time *15 minutes* serves *4*
nutritional count per serving *0.3g total fat (0g saturated fat); 598kJ (143 cal); 30g carbohydrate; 1.6g protein; 6.1g fibre*

salad dressings

321

rocket & garlic mayonnaise, page 324

It's worthwhile to learn how to make a few salad dressings – even iceberg lettuce can be raised to great heights with a good dressing – and you'll never go back to bought dressings once you've made your own.

323

rocket & garlic mayonnaise

1 cup (300g) mayonnaise
50g baby rocket leaves, trimmed
1 clove garlic, crushed
1 teaspoon finely grated lemon rind

1 Blend or process ingredients until smooth.

prep time *10 minutes* makes *1¼ cup (310ml)*
nutritional count per tablespoon *24.1g total fat (2.9g
saturated fat); 1162kJ (278 cal); 14.7g carbohydrate;
1g protein; 0.8g fibre*

green goddess dressing

1 cup (300g) mayonnaise
2 drained anchovy fillets, chopped finely
2 green onions, sliced thinly
2 teaspoons finely chopped fresh flat-leaf parsley
2 teaspoons finely chopped fresh chives
2 teaspoons finely chopped fresh tarragon
2 teaspoons cider vinegar

1 Combine ingredients in small bowl.

prep time *10 minutes* makes *1¼ cup (310ml)*
nutritional count per tablespoon *24.2g total fat (2.9g
saturated fat); 1166kJ (279 cal); 14.6g carbohydrate;
1.2g protein; 0.6g fibre*

green goddess dressing

ginger miso dressing

classic italian dressing

classic french dressing

red berry vinaigrette

ginger miso dressing

¼ cup (60ml) rice vinegar
2 tablespoons white miso
1 tablespoon mirin
2 teaspoons caster sugar
2cm piece fresh ginger (10g), grated
1 clove garlic, crushed
1 teaspoon soy sauce
1 teaspoon sesame oil
1 tablespoon water

1 Stir ingredients in small saucepan, over low heat, until sugar dissolves.

2 Remove pan from heat, strain over small jug; discard solids.

prep & cook time 20 minutes makes ½ cup (125ml) nutritional count per tablespoon 1.3g total fat (0.2g saturated fat); 125kJ (30 cal); 3.3g carbohydrate; 1.0g protein; 0.6g fibre

classic french dressing

¼ cup (60ml) white vinegar
¾ cup (180ml) olive oil
½ teaspoon sugar
1 teaspoon dijon mustard

1 Place ingredients in screw-top jar; shake well.

prep time 10 minutes makes about 1 cup (250ml) nutritional count per tablespoon 13.7g total fat (1.9g saturated fat); 506kJ (121 cal); 0.2g carbohydrate; 0g protein; 0g fibre

classic italian dressing

2 tablespoons white wine vinegar
2 tablespoons lemon juice
½ teaspoon sugar
2 cloves garlic, crushed
¾ cup (180ml) olive oil
1 tablespoon finely chopped fresh basil leaves
1 tablespoon finely chopped fresh oregano leaves

1 Place ingredients in screw-top jar; shake well.

prep time 10 minutes makes about 1 cup (250ml) nutritional count per tablespoon 13.7g total fat (1.9g saturated fat); 510kJ (122 cal); 0.3g carbohydrate; 0.1g protein; 0.1g fibre

red berry vinaigrette

¼ cup (60ml) red wine vinegar
½ cup (125ml) olive oil
150g fresh raspberries
¼ cup (80g) whole berry cranberry sauce

1 Blend or process ingredients until smooth.

2 Push dressing through fine sieve into small bowl.

prep time 5 minutes makes 1 cup (250ml) nutritional count per tablespoon 9.5g total fat (1.3g saturated fat); 418kJ (100 cal); 3.4g carbohydrate; 0.2g protein; 0.7g fibre

Use raspberry vinegar in place of red wine vinegar for an extra fruity taste. If dressing is too thick, stir in a little cold water until dressing is of desired consistency.

oregano & caper dressing

2 hard-boiled eggs, quartered
1 tablespoon drained capers, rinsed
2 tablespoons white wine vinegar
2 tablespoons coarsely chopped fresh oregano
1 clove garlic, quartered
⅓ cup (80ml) olive oil

1 Blend or process egg, capers, vinegar, oregano and garlic until smooth.
2 With motor operating, add oil in a thin, steady stream; blend until dressing thickens.

prep time *10 minutes* makes *1 cup (250ml)*
nutritional count per tablespoon *7g total fat (1.1g saturated fat); 280kJ (67 cal); 0.2g carbohydrate; 1.1g protein; 0.1g fibre*

rosemary balsamic dressing

2 tablespoons olive oil
1 tablespoon balsamic vinegar
1 tablespoon lemon juice
1 tablespoon coarsely chopped fresh rosemary

1 Place ingredients in screw-top jar; shake well.

prep time *10 minutes* makes *⅓ cup (80ml)*
nutritional count per tablespoon *9.1g total fat (1.3g saturated fat); 339kJ (81 cal); 0.1g carbohydrate; 0g protein; 0g fibre*

thousand island dressing

½ cup (150g) mayonnaise
1½ tablespoons tomato sauce
½ small white onion (40g), grated finely
8 pimiento-stuffed green olives, chopped finely
½ small red capsicum (75g), chopped finely

1 Combine ingredients in small bowl.

prep time *10 minutes* makes *1 cup (250ml)*
nutritional count per tablespoon *4.3g total fat (0.5g saturated fat); 226kJ (54 cal); 3.6g carbohydrate; 0.3g protein; 0.4g fibre*

sweet chilli dressing

2 tablespoons fish sauce
2 tablespoons sweet chilli sauce
⅓ cup (80ml) lime juice
1 fresh long red chilli, chopped finely
1 tablespoon grated palm sugar

1 Place ingredients in screw-top jar; shake well.

prep time *5 minutes* makes *⅔ cup (160ml)*
nutritional count per tablespoon *0.1g total fat (0g saturated fat); 71kJ (17 cal); 3g carbohydrate; 0.6g protein; 0.3g fibre*

oregano & caper dressing

thousand island dressing

rosemary balsamic dressing

sweet chilli dressing

macadamia dressing

american ranch dressing

citrus & poppy seed dressing

classic mayonnaise

macadamia dressing

½ cup (125ml) macadamia oil
⅓ cup (45g) finely chopped roasted unsalted
    macadamias
2 teaspoons finely grated lemon rind
2 tablespoons lemon juice
1 teaspoon caster sugar

1 Whisk ingredients in small jug until combined.

prep time *10 minutes* makes *1 cup (250ml)*
nutritional count per tablespoon *12.4g total fat*
(1.8g saturated fat); 477kJ (114 cal); 0.6g carbohydrate;
0.3g protein; 0.2g fibre

citrus & poppy seed dressing

2 teaspoons finely grated orange rind
¼ cup (60ml) orange juice
2 tablespoons cider vinegar
1 tablespoon poppy seeds
⅓ cup (80g) sour cream
2 teaspoons honey mustard
¼ cup (60ml) water

1 Whisk rind, juice, vinegar, seeds, sour cream and
mustard in small bowl. Add the water; whisk until
combined.

prep time *10 minutes* makes *1 cup (250ml)*
nutritional count per tablespoon *3.1g total fat*
(1.8g saturated fat); 134kJ (32 cal); 0.7g carbohydrate;
0.4g protein; 0.2g fibre

american ranch dressing

½ cup (150g) mayonnaise
¼ cup (60ml) buttermilk
1 tablespoon white wine vinegar
1 small brown onion (80g), chopped finely
1 clove garlic, crushed
1 tablespoon finely chopped fresh chives
1 tablespoon finely chopped fresh flat-leaf parsley
¼ teaspoon sweet paprika

1 Whisk ingredients in small jug until combined.

prep time *10 minutes* makes *1 cup (250ml)*
nutritional count per tablespoon *4.2g total fat*
(0.5g saturated fat); 217kJ (52 cal); 3.2g carbohydrate;
0.5g protein; 0.2g fibre

classic mayonnaise

2 egg yolks
½ teaspoon salt
1 teaspoon dijon mustard
⅔ cup (160ml) extra light olive oil
⅓ cup (80ml) olive oil
1 tablespoon white wine vinegar
1 tablespoon lemon juice

1 Combine egg yolks, salt and mustard in medium bowl.
Gradually add oils in a thin, steady stream, whisking constantly
until mixture thickens. Stir in vinegar and juice.

prep time *15 minutes* makes *1 cup (250ml)*
nutritional count per tablespoon *19.2g total fat*
(2.9g saturated fat); 719kJ (172 cal); 0g carbohydrate;
0.5g protein; 0g fibre

lemon & chive vinaigrette

2 cloves garlic, crushed
¼ cup (60ml) white wine vinegar
1 tablespoon finely chopped preserved lemon rind
½ cup (125ml) olive oil
1 tablespoon coarsely chopped fresh chives

1 Place garlic, vinegar, rind and oil in screw-top jar; shake well. Add chives.

prep time *10 minutes*   makes *¾ cup (180ml)*
nutritional count per tablespoon *9.5g total fat (1.3g saturated fat); 355kJ (85 cal); 0.1g carbohydrate; 0.1g protein; 0.1g fibre*

Rinse preserved lemon under cold water; cut flesh away and discard it, using only the rind.

classic russian dressing

1 large beetroot (200g), trimmed
2 tablespoons coarsely chopped pickled onions
1 tablespoon drained capers, rinsed
½ cup (120g) sour cream

1 Boil, steam or microwave unpeeled beetroot until tender; drain, reserving ¼ cup of the cooking liquid. When cool enough to handle, peel then chop beetroot coarsely.

2 Blend or process beetroot with remaining ingredients and reserved liquid until smooth.

prep & cook time *35 minutes*   makes *1½ cup (375ml)*
nutritional count per tablespoon *14g total fat (9.2g saturated fat); 681kJ (163 cal); 7g carbohydrate; 1.8g protein; 1.8g fibre*

A small can of beetroot, drained and chopped, can be used instead of fresh beetroot.

sesame soy dressing

1 tablespoon toasted sesame seeds
1 tablespoon sesame oil
2 shallots (50g), chopped finely
1 tablespoon kecap manis
¼ cup (60ml) lime juice

1 Combine ingredients in small bowl.

prep time *5 minutes*   makes *½ cup (125ml)*
nutritional count per tablespoon *1.4g total fat (0.2g saturated fat); 63kJ (15 cal); 0.2g carbohydrate; 0.3g protein; 0.1g fibre*

watercress dressing

1 teaspoon caster sugar
⅓ cup (80ml) cider vinegar
1 cup (250ml) olive oil
350g watercress, trimmed, chopped coarsely

1 Blend or process ingredients until smooth.

prep time *5 minutes*   makes *2 cups (500ml)*
nutritional count per tablespoon *9.5g total fat (1.3g saturated fat); 372kJ (89 cal); 0.3g carbohydrate; 0.4g protein; 0.6g fibre*

lemon & chive vinaigrette

sesame soy dressing

classic russian dressing

watercress dressing

orange & chilli vinaigrette

lemon myrtle dressing

classic pesto dressing

balsamic & garlic dressing

orange & chilli vinaigrette

1 cup (250ml) orange juice
1 fresh long red chilli, chopped coarsely
1 teaspoon finely grated orange rind
2 teaspoons dijon mustard
½ cup (125ml) olive oil

1 Place juice in small saucepan; simmer, uncovered, about 10 minutes or until liquid reduces to a third of a cup. Add chilli and rind; cool to room temperature.

2 Blend or process juice mixture with mustard until smooth. With motor operating, gradually add oil in thin, steady stream; process until dressing thickens.

prep & cook time *15 minutes (+ cooling)*
makes *1 cup (250ml)*
nutritional count per tablespoon *9.5g total fat (1.3g saturated fat); 385kJ (92 cal); 1.8g carbohydrate; 0.2g protein; 0.1g fibre*

classic pesto dressing

2 cloves garlic, crushed
¼ cup (20g) finely grated parmesan cheese
1 tablespoon roasted pine nuts
1 tablespoon lemon juice
1 cup firmly packed fresh basil leaves
⅓ cup (80ml) olive oil
½ cup (125ml) buttermilk

1 Blend or process garlic, cheese, nuts, juice, basil and oil until smooth.

2 Transfer basil mixture to small bowl; stir in buttermilk.

prep time *10 minutes* makes *1 cup (250ml)*
nutritional count per tablespoon *7.7g total fat (1.4g saturated fat); 322kJ (77 cal); 0.8g carbohydrate; 1.3g protein; 0.2g fibre*

lemon myrtle dressing

¼ cup (60ml) cider vinegar
2 tablespoons lemon juice
2 teaspoons ground lemon myrtle
½ cup (125ml) macadamia oil
⅓ cup (45g) finely chopped roasted macadamias

1 Whisk vinegar, juice and lemon myrtle in small bowl until combined.

2 Gradually add oil in thin, steady stream, whisking constantly until combined. Stir in nuts.

prep time *15 minutes* makes *1 cup (250ml)*
nutritional count per tablespoon *12.5g total fat (1.8g saturated fat); 477kJ (114 cal); 0.3g carbohydrate; 0.3g protein; 0.2g fibre*

Ground lemon myrtle is available from specialist spice shops and some gourmet food stores. Lemon myrtle is a small tree that grows in sub-tropical and tropical rainforest areas of Queensland. Ground lemon myrtle is a ground mixture of the dried leaf and flower; it has a strong lemon flavour. If you can't find it, use 2 teaspoons finely grated lemon rind instead.

balsamic & garlic dressing

2 tablespoons balsamic vinegar
¼ cup (60ml) lemon juice
1 clove garlic, crushed
¾ cup (180ml) olive oil

1 Whisk ingredients in small bowl until combined.

prep time *5 minutes* makes *1¼ cups (310ml)*
nutritional count per tablespoon *10.9g total fat (1.5g saturated fat); 406kJ (97 cal); 0.1g carbohydrate; 0g protein; 0g fibre*

glossary

Allspice also known as pimento or jamaican pepper; so-named because it tastes like a combination of nutmeg, cumin, clove and cinnamon. Available whole or ground.

Almonds *see nuts*

Artichoke heart tender centre of the globe artichoke; harvested from the plant after the prickly choke is removed. Buy from delicatessens or canned in brine.

Baba ghanoush a roasted eggplant (aubergine) dip or spread.

Bacon
rashers also known as bacon slices; made from cured and smoked pork side.
shortcut a "half rasher"; the streaky (belly), narrow portion of the rasher has been removed leaving the choice cut eye meat (large end).
streaky is the fatty end of a bacon rasher without the lean (eye) meat.

Basil *see herbs; see also page 11*

Beans
borlotti also called roman beans or pink beans, can be eaten fresh or dried. Interchangeable with pinto beans due to their similarity in appearance – pale pink or beige with dark red streaks.
broad also known as fava, windsor and horse beans; available dried, fresh, canned and frozen. Fresh and frozen forms should be peeled twice (discarding both the outer long green pod and the beige-green tough inner shell).
butter cans labelled butter beans are, in fact, cannellini beans. Confusingly butter is also another name for lima beans,

sold both dried and canned; a large beige bean having a mealy texture and mild taste.
cannellini small white bean similar in appearance and flavour to other phaseolus vulgaris varieties (great northern, navy or haricot). Available dried or canned.
dried black also known as turtle beans or black kidney beans; an earthy-flavoured dried bean completely different from the better-known chinese black beans (which are fermented soya beans).
four-bean mix consists of kidney beans, butter beans, chickpeas and cannellini beans.
green also known as french or string beans; this long thin fresh bean is consumed in its entirety once cooked.
kidney medium-sized red bean, slightly floury in texture yet sweet in flavour; sold dried or canned.
lima large, flat kidney-shaped, beige dried and canned beans. Also known as butter beans.
snake long (about 40cm), thin, round, fresh green beans, Asian in origin, with a taste similar to green or french beans. Used most frequently in stir-fries, they are also known as yard-long beans because of their (pre-metric) length.
sprouts also known as bean shoots; tender new shoots of assorted beans and seeds germinated for consumption as sprouts (including mung beans, soya beans, alfalfa and snow pea sprouts). *see also page 13*
white in this book, some recipes may simply call for "white beans", a generic term we use for canned or dried cannellini, haricot, navy or great northern beans.

Beef
calves liver tender with a fine texture and delicious taste; has a better flavour than beef liver.
eye-fillet tenderloin fillet; an expensive cut of meat with a fine texture.
fillet a generic name given to a steak cut from the tenderloin.
minute very thin boneless beef, usually scored and pounded to tenderise it.
new-york cut boneless striploin steak.
rump boneless tender cut taken from the hindquarter.
scotch fillet cut from the muscle running behind the shoulder along the spine. Also known as cube roll; cuts include standing rib roast and rib-eye.
sirloin cut from the lower portion of the ribs, continuing off the tenderloin, from which filet mignon is cut.
skirt steak lean, flavourful coarse-grained cut.
t-bone sirloin steak with the bone in and eye fillet attached.

Beetroot also known as red beets or beets; a firm, round root vegetable.

Bicarbonate of soda also known as baking or carb soda; a mild alkali used as a leavening agent in baking.

Bocconcini cheese *see cheese*

Breads
ciabatta in Italian, the word means slipper, which is the traditional shape of this popular white bread with a crisp crust.
flat breads also known as roti, chapatti, phulka and parantha. Made of wheat and water and used for scooping or wrapping.
focaccia a popular Italian flat, yeast bread. The top is dimpled

and brushed with oil to keep the bread moist and flavourful. The most basic focaccia is simply a herbed and oiled bread with salt, but the variations are endless.
french stick also known as french bread, french loaf or baguette; formed into a long, narrow cylindrical loaf with a crisp brown crust and light chewy interior. A standard french stick is 5-6cm wide and 3-4cm tall, but can be up to a metre in length.
lavash flat, unleavened bread of Mediterranean origin.
pitta also known as lebanese bread. This wheat-flour pocket bread is sold in large, flat pieces that separate into two thin rounds. Also available in small pieces called pocket pitta.
sourdough so-named, not because it's sour in taste, but because it's made by using a small amount of "starter dough", which contains a yeast culture, mixed into flour and water. Part of the resulting dough is then saved to use as the starter dough next time.
tortilla thin, round, unleavened bread originating in Mexico. Two kinds are available, one made from wheat flour and the other from corn.
turkish also known as pide; comes in long (about 45cm) flat loaves as well as individual rounds. Made from wheat flour and sprinkled with sesame seeds or kalonji (black onion seeds).

Breadcrumbs
fresh bread, usually white, processed into crumbs.
japanese also called ponko; available in two kinds: larger pieces and fine crumbs; have a lighter texture than Western-style ones. Available from Asian food stores and some supermarkets.

packaged prepared fine-textured, but crunchy, white breadcrumbs.

stale made by processing one- or two-day-old bread.

Brie cheese *see cheese*

Broccolini a cross between broccoli and chinese kale; has long asparagus-like stems with a long loose floret, both completely edible. Resembles broccoli in look but is milder and sweeter in taste.

Buk choy also known as bok choy, pak choi, chinese white cabbage or chinese chard; has a fresh, mild mustard taste. Baby buk choy, also known as pak kat farang or shanghai bok choy, is much smaller and more tender than buk choy.

Burghul also known as bulghur or bulgar wheat; hulled steamed wheat kernels that, once dried, are crushed into various size grains. Not the same as cracked wheat. Found in health food stores or most supermarkets.

Butter use salted or unsalted (sweet) butter; 125g is equal to one stick (4 ounces) of butter.

Buttermilk originally the term given to the slightly sour liquid left after butter was churned from cream, today it is made similarly to yogurt. Found in the refrigerated section in supermarkets. Despite its name, it is low in fat.

Camembert cheese *see cheese*

Caperberries fruit formed after the caper buds have flowered; caperberries are pickled, usually with their stalks intact.

Capers the grey-green buds of a warm climate shrub (usually Mediterranean); sold either dried and salted, or pickled in a vinegar brine. Baby capers are smaller, fuller-flavoured and more expensive than the full-sized ones. Capers should be rinsed well before using.

Capsicum also known as bell pepper or, simply, pepper. Come in many colours: red, green, yellow, orange and purplish-black. Discard seeds and membranes before use.

Caraway seeds have a sweetly rich flavour; available in seed or ground form.

Cardamom has a distinctive, aromatic, sweetly rich flavour; is one of the world's most expensive spices. Available in pod, seed or ground form.

Cashews *see nuts*

Cheese

bocconcini from "boccone", meaning mouthful in Italian; a walnut-sized baby mozzarella. Is a delicate, semi-soft, white cheese. Sold fresh, it spoils rapidly so will only keep for one or two days refrigerated in brine.

brie often referred to in France as the queen of cheeses; soft-ripened cow-milk cheese with a delicate, creamy texture and a rich, sweet taste that varies from buttery to mushroomy.

camembert made from cows' milk. Has a creamy yellow flesh encased in a speckled, floury, mouldy-looking crust. A ripe camembert is six weeks old with a fruity, tangy fragrance.

cheddar the most common cows-milk tasty cheese; should be aged, hard and have a pronounced bite.

cream commonly known as Philadelphia or Philly; a soft cows-milk cheese. Also available as spreadable light cream cheese, which is a blend of cottage and cream cheeses.

fetta a crumbly textured goat- or sheep-milk cheese having a sharp, salty taste. Ripened and stored in salted whey.

fontina a smooth, firm cows-milk cheese with a creamy, nutty taste and brown or red rind.

goats made from goats milk; has an earthy, strong taste. Available in soft, crumbly and firm textures, in various shapes and sizes, and sometimes rolled in ash or herbs.

haloumi has a semi-firm, spongy texture and very salty yet sweet flavour. Ripened and stored in salted whey, it holds its shape well when heated. Best eaten while still warm as it becomes rubbery when cool.

mascarpone an ivory-coloured, buttery-rich, cream-like cheese made from cows' milk; most often used in desserts.

mozzarella soft, spun-curd cheese; most popular pizza cheese because of its low melting point and elasticity when heated.

parmesan also known as parmigiana; a hard, grainy cows-milk cheese.

pecorino the generic name for cheeses made from sheep milk. Is a hard, white to pale yellow cheese; if you can't find it, use parmesan.

ricotta a soft, white, sweet, cows-milk cheese having a slightly grainy texture. The name roughly translates as "cooked again" and refers to ricotta's manufacture from a whey that is itself a by-product of other cheese making.

roquefort considered the "king of cheeses", this is a blue cheese with a singularly pungent taste; made only from the milk of specially bred sheep and ripened in the damp limestone caves found under the village of Roquefort-sur-Soulzon in France. Has a sticky, bone-coloured rind and, when ripe, the sharp, almost metallic-tasting interior is creamy and almost shiny.

Chervil *see herbs; see also page 11*

Chickpeas also known as channa, garbanzos or hummus; an irregularly round, sandy-coloured legume.

Chilli always use rubber gloves when seeding and chopping fresh chillies as they can burn your skin. We use unseeded chillies in our recipes because the seeds contain the heat; use fewer chillies rather than seeding the lot.

cayenne pepper extremely hot, long, thin-fleshed, dried red chilli, usually purchased ground; both arbol and guajillo chillies are the fresh sources for cayenne.

chipotle (cheh-pote-lay) the name used for jalapeño chillies once they've been dried and smoked. Has a deep, intensely smoky flavour, rather than a searing heat; are dark brown, almost black in colour and wrinkled in appearance.

flakes also sold as crushed chilli; dehydrated deep-red extremely fine slices and whole seeds.

green any unripened chilli; also some particular varieties that are ripe when green, such as jalapeño, habanero, poblano or serrano.

jalapeño fairly hot green chilli, available in brine, bottled, or fresh from greengrocers.

long red available both fresh and dried; a generic term used for any moderately hot, long, thin chilli (6-8cm long).

pasilla (pah-see-yah) also known as "chile negro" because of its almost black skin; pungent, medium-hot, smoky, dried chilli measuring about 15cm to 20cm in length. Use sparingly until you discover the right amount for your palate.

pickled green green chillies available pickled in vinegar and sugar; from Asian grocery stores and some delicatessens.

powder the Asian variety is the hottest, made from dried ground thai red chillies; can be used instead of fresh chillies in the proportion of ½ teaspoon chilli powder to 1 medium chopped fresh red chilli.

red thai also known as "scuds"; tiny, hot and bright red in colour.

Chinese barbecued duck *see poultry*

Chinese barbecued pork *see pork*

Chinese cooking wine also called chinese rice wine or shao hsing; made from fermented rice, wheat, sugar and salt. Inexpensive and found in Asian grocery stores; if you can't find it, use mirin or sherry, instead.

Chives related to the onion and leek; has a subtle onion flavour. *see also page 11*

Chorizo sausages *see sausages*

Choy sum also known as pakaukeo or flowering cabbage, a member of the buk choy family; easy to identify with its long stems, light green leaves and yellow flowers. Stems and leaves are both edible, steamed or stir-fried.

Cinnamon dried inner bark of the shoots of the cinnamon tree; available in stick (quill) or ground form.

Coconut
cream obtained from the first pressing of the coconut flesh alone, without the addition of water. Available in cans and cartons at supermarkets.
flaked dried and flaked flesh of the coconut.

fresh to open a fresh coconut, pierce one of the eyes then roast briefly in a very hot oven only until cracks appear in the shell. Cool then break it apart and grate or flake the firm white flesh.
milk not the liquid found inside the fruit (called coconut water), but the diluted liquid from the second pressing of the white flesh of a mature coconut. Available in cans and cartons at most supermarkets.

Coriander also known as pak chee, cilantro or chinese parsley; bright-green leafy herb with a pungent flavour. Both the stems and roots of coriander are used; wash well before using. Coriander seeds are also available but are no substitute for fresh coriander, as the taste is very different. *see also page 11*

Couscous a fine, grain-like cereal product made from semolina. A semolina flour and water dough is sieved then dehydrated to produce minuscule even-sized pellets of couscous; it is rehydrated by steaming, or with the addition of a warm liquid, and swells to three or four times its original size.

Cranberries, dried have the same slightly sour, succulent flavour as fresh cranberries. Available in supermarkets and health-food stores.

Cream we used fresh cream, unless otherwise stated. Also known as pure cream and pouring cream.
crème fraîche fermented cream with a tangy, nutty flavour and velvety texture.
sour a thick commercially-cultured soured cream. Light sour cream is also available.
thickened a whipping cream containing a thickener.

Cumin also known as zeera or comino; has a spicy, nutty flavour. Available in seed, dried and ground forms.

Currants, dried tiny, almost black raisins so-named after a grape variety that originated in Corinth, Greece.

Curry pastes
balti a medium-hot, aromatic paste containing coriander, fenugreek and mint, which gives it its distinctive mild "green" flavour.
green the hottest of the traditional pastes containing green chilli, garlic, shallot, lemon grass, salt, galangal, shrimp paste, kaffir lime peel, coriander seed, pepper, cumin and turmeric.
rogan josh a paste of medium heat, made from fresh chillies or paprika, tomato and spices, especially cardamom.
tandoori paste consisting of garlic, tamarind, ginger, chilli, coriander and various spices.

Curry powder a blend of ground spices used for making Indian and some South-East Asian dishes. Consists of some of the following spices: dried chilli, cinnamon, coriander, cumin, fennel, fenugreek, mace, cardamom and turmeric. Available mild or hot.

Daikon also known as giant white radish; has a sweet, fresh flavour without the bite of the common red radish.Used raw or cooked.

Dill also known as dill weed; used fresh or dried, in seed form or ground. Has an anise/celery sweetness; its distinctive feathery, frond-like fresh leaves are grassier and more subtle than the dried version or the seeds. *see also page 11*

Dukkah an Egyptian specialty made from various roasted nuts and spices. Dip bread into olive oil and then dip it into the dukkah for a tasty snack.

Eggplant also known as aubergine. Ranges in size from tiny to large, and in colour from pale-green to deep-purple. Also available char-grilled, packed in oil, in jars. Baby eggplant, also known as japanese or finger eggplant, are small and slender.

Fennel also known as finocchio or anise; a white to very pale green-white, firm, crisp, roundish vegetable about 8-12cm in diameter. The bulb has a slightly

sweet, anise flavour but the leaves have a much stronger taste. Also the name given to dried seeds having a licorice flavour.

Fetta *see cheese*

Figs vary in skin and flesh colour according to type, not ripeness. When ripe, should be unblemished and bursting with flesh; nectar beads at the base indicate when it's at its best.

Fish sauce *see sauces*

Five-spice powder a fragrant mixture of cinnamon, cloves, star anise, sichuan pepper and fennel seeds. Also known as chinese five-spice.

Flour
plain an all-purpose flour, made from wheat.
self-raising plain flour sifted with baking powder in the proportion of 1 cup flour to 2 teaspoons baking powder.

Fontina *see cheese*

Gai lan also called chinese broccoli, gai larn, kanah, gai lum and chinese kale; used more for its stems than its coarse leaves.

Ginger
fresh also known as green or root ginger; the thick gnarled root of a tropical plant.
ground also called powdered ginger; used as a flavouring in baking but cannot be substituted for fresh ginger.
pickled pink or red coloured; available, packaged, from Asian food shops. Pickled paper-thin shavings of ginger in a mixture of vinegar, sugar and natural colouring; used in Japanese cooking.

Goats cheese *see cheese*

Gow gee wrappers *see wonton wrappers*

Haloumi *see cheese*

Harissa paste a Moroccan sauce or paste made from dried chillies, cumin, garlic, oil and caraway seeds. It is available in supermarkets and Middle-Eastern grocery stores.

Hazelnuts *see nuts*

Herbs

basil there are many types, but the most commonly used basil in cooking is sweet, or common, basil. *see also page 11*
thai also known as horapa; has smallish leaves and a sweet licorice/aniseed taste. Available from Asian grocery stores, major supermarkets and greengrocers. *see also page 11*
chervil also known as cicily; mildly fennel-flavoured herb with curly dark-green leaves. *see also page 11*
flat-leaf parsley also known as continental or italian parsley. *see also page 10*
marjoram an aromatic herb that is a member of the mint family; has long, thin, oval-shaped, pale-green leaves and a sweet taste similar to oregano. Used fresh or dried.
mint the most commonly used variety of mint is spearmint; it has pointed, bright-green leaves and a fresh flavour. *see also page 10.*
oregano a herb having a woody stalk with clumps of tiny, dark green leaves with a pungent, peppery flavour. Can be used fresh or dried; also known as wild marjoram. *see also page 10*
tarragon an aromatic herb with dark green leaves and an anise-like flavour. *see also page 11*
thyme a member of the mint family; there are many types of this herb but we most often use the "household" variety known as french thyme, or simply called thyme in most shops. It has tiny grey-green leaves that give off a pungent minty, light-lemon aroma. *see also page 11*
lemon thyme a herb with a lemony scent, which is due to the high level of citral in its leaves – an oil also found in lemon, orange, verbena and lemon grass. The citrus scent is enhanced by crushing the leaves in your hands before using the herb. *see also page 11*
vietnamese mint not a mint at all, but a pungent and peppery narrow-leafed member of the buckwheat family; also called cambodian mint or laksa leaf. *see also page 10*

Hoisin sauce *see sauces*

Honeydew a heavy oval fruit with a pale-green to yellow skin, delicate taste and pale green flesh.

Horseradish there are two commercially prepared horseradish products on the market – cream and prepared. These cannot be substituted one for the other in cooking but both can be used as table condiments.
cream a creamy paste that consists of grated horseradish, vinegar, oil and sugar.
prepared the preserved grated root.

Hummus a Middle Eastern salad or dip made from garlic, chickpeas, lemon juice and tahini (sesame seed paste); available from supermarkets.

Kaffir lime also known as magrood, leech lime or jeruk purut. The wrinkled, bumpy-skinned green fruit of a small citrus tree originally grown in South Africa and South-East Asia. As a rule, only the rind and leaves are used.

Kaffir lime leaves also known as bai magrood; sold fresh, dried or frozen. Looks like two glossy dark green leaves joined end to end, forming a rounded hourglass shape. Dried leaves are less potent, so double the number called for in a recipe if you substitute them for fresh. A strip of fresh lime peel may be substituted for each kaffir lime leaf.

Kecap manis *see sauces*

Kiwifruit also known as chinese gooseberry. Has a brown, somewhat hairy skin and bright-green or gold flesh with a sweet-tart flavour.

Kumara Polynesian name of orange-fleshed sweet potato often confused with yam.

Lamb
backstrap also known as eye of loin; the larger fillet from a row of loin chops or cutlets.
boned rolled loin loin that has had the bone removed.

chump cut from just above the hind legs to the mid-loin section; used for roasting or cut into chops.
cutlet small, tender rib chop.
diced cubed lean meat.
fillet extremely expensive, fine textured and very tender piece of tenderloin.
leg cut from the hindquarter.
loin chop cut from the back of the lamb; a tender, but expensive, cut.

Lebanese cucumber short, slender and thin-skinned. Probably the most popular variety because of its tender, edible skin, tiny, yielding seeds and sweet, fresh taste.

Leek a member of the onion family; looks like a large green onion but is more subtle and mild in flavour. Wash well before use. Pencil leeks, young, slender leeks, can be cooked and eaten like asparagus.

Lemon grass a tall, clumping, lemon-smelling and -tasting, sharp-edged grass; the white part of each stem is chopped and used in Asian cooking.

Lemon pepper also known as lemon pepper seasoning; a blend of crushed black pepper, lemon, herbs and spices.

Lemon thyme *see herbs; see also page 11*

Lentils (red, brown, yellow) dried pulses often identified by, and named after, their colour.

Lettuce and salad greens
asian greens a mix of baby buk choy, choy sum, gai lan and water spinach. Store in the refrigerator and use within 1-2 days of buying.
butter small, round, loosely formed heads with a sweet flavour; soft, buttery-textured leaves range from pale green on the outer leaves to pale yellow-green inner leaves. *see also page 12*
cos also known as romaine lettuce; the traditional caesar salad lettuce. Long, with leaves ranging from dark green on the outside to almost white near the core; the leaves have a stiff centre rib that gives a slight cupping effect to the leaf on either side. *see also page 12*
curly endive also known as frisée, a curly-leafed green vegetable; used in salads. *see also page 13*
iceberg a heavy, firm lettuce with tightly packed leaves and a crisp texture; the most common "family" lettuce used on sandwiches and in salads. *see also page 12*
lamb's lettuce also known as mâche, corn salad or lamb tongue, the tender narrow dark-green leaves have a mild, almost nutty flavour. *see also page 13*
mesclun also known as salad mix or gourmet salad mix; a mixture of assorted young lettuce and other green leaves, including baby spinach leaves, mizuna and curly endive. *see also page 12*
mizuna a wispy, feathered mild-tasting green salad leaf. *see also page 12*
oak leaf also known as feuille de chene; curly-leafed but not as frizzy as the coral lettuce. Found in both red and green varieties. *see also page 12*
radicchio a member of the chicory family. The dark burgundy leaves have a strong, bitter flavour; can be cooked or eaten raw in salads. *see also page 12*
rocket also known as arugula, rugula and rucola; a peppery-tasting green leaf. Baby rocket leaves (also known as wild rocket) are both smaller and less peppery. *see also page 12*
witlof also known as chicory or belgian endive; cigar-shaped with tightly packed heads and pale, yellow-green tips. Has a slight bitter flavour. *see also page 13*

Lime pickle an Indian special mixed pickle/condiment of limes that adds a hot and spicy taste to meals, especially rice. Available in Indian food shops.

Lychees a small fruit from China with a hard shell and sweet, juicy flesh. The white flesh has a gelatinous texture and musky, perfumed taste. Discard the rough skin and seed before using in salads or as a dessert fruit. Also available canned in a sugar syrup.

Macadamia *see nuts*

Mandarin small, loose-skinned citrus fruit also known as tangerine. Segments in a light syrup are available canned.

Mango tropical fruit with skin colour ranging from green through yellow to deep red. Fragrant deep-yellow flesh surrounds a large flat seed. Mango cheeks in a light syrup are available canned.
green sour and crunchy green mangoes are just immature fruit. Often available from Asian grocery stores.

Maple syrup a thin syrup distilled from the sap of the maple tree. Maple-flavoured syrup or pancake syrup is not an adequate substitute for the real thing.

Maple-flavoured syrup is made from sugar cane and is also known as golden or pancake syrup. It is not a substitute for pure maple syrup.

Marjoram *see herbs*

Mascarpone *see cheese*

Mayonnaise a rich, creamy dressing made with egg yolks, vegetable oil, mustard and vinegar or lemon juice. We prefer to use whole egg mayonnaise in our recipes.

Mince also known as ground meat, as in beef, veal, lamb, pork and chicken.

Mint *see herbs; see also page 10*

Mirin a champagne-coloured cooking wine from Japan; made of glutinous rice and alcohol and used only for cooking. Do not confuse with drinking sake.

Mixed spice a classic spice mixture generally containing caraway, allspice, coriander, cumin, nutmeg and ginger, although cinnamon and other spices can be added. It is used with fruit and in cakes.

Mozzarella *see cheese*

Mushrooms
button small, cultivated white mushrooms with a mild flavour.
enoki clumps of long, spaghetti-like stems with tiny, snowy-white caps.
flat large, flat mushrooms with a rich, earthy flavour. Are sometimes misnamed field mushrooms, which are wild mushrooms.
oyster also known as abalone; grey-white mushroom shaped like a fan. Prized for their smooth texture and subtle, oyster-like flavour.
shiitake when fresh are also known as chinese black, forest or golden oak mushrooms; although cultivated, they have the earthiness and taste of wild mushrooms. Are large and meaty. When dried, they are also known as donko or dried chinese mushrooms; rehydrate before use.
swiss brown also called cremini or roman mushrooms; are light brown mushrooms having a full-bodied flavour. Button or cup mushrooms can be substituted.

Mustard
american-style bright yellow in colour; a sweet mustard made from mustard seeds, sugar, salt, spices and garlic. *see also page 10*
dijon a pale brown, fairly mild french mustard. *see also page 10*
powder finely ground white (yellow) mustard seeds.
seeds, yellow also known as white mustard seeds; used ground for mustard powder and in most prepared mustards.
wholegrain also known as seeded. A french-style coarse-grain mustard made from crushed mustard seeds and dijon-style french mustard. *see also page 10*

Nashi a member if the pear family but resembling an apple with its pale-yellow-green, tennis-ball-sized appearance; more commonly known as the asian pear to much of the world The nashi is different from other pears in that it is crisp, juicy and ready to eat as soon as it is picked and for several months thereafter, unlike its European cousins. These very qualities are more apple- than pear-like, which probably accounts for the widespread misconception that the nashi is a cross between an apple and a pear. Its distinctive texture and mildly sweet taste make it perfect for use raw in salads, or as part of a cheese platter.

Noodles
fresh rice also known as ho fun, khao pun, sen yau, pho or kway tiau. Can be purchased in strands of various widths or large sheets weighing about 500g, which are then cut into the noodle size required. Chewy and pure white, they do not need pre-cooking before use.
fried crispy egg noodles that have been deep-fried then packaged for sale on supermarket shelves.
rice vermicelli also known as sen mee, mei fun or bee hoon. Made with rice flour. Before using, soak dried noodles in hot water until softened, boil them briefly then rinse with hot water.
soba thin, pale-brown noodle originally from Japan; made from buckwheat and varying proportions of wheat flour. Available dried and fresh, and in flavoured (for instance, green tea) varieties; eaten in soups, stir-fries and, chilled, on their own.

Nori a type of dried seaweed used in Japanese cooking as a flavouring, garnish or for sushi. Sold in thin sheets, plain or toasted (yaki-nori).

Nutmeg the dried nut of an evergreen tree native to Indonesia; it is available in ground form or you can grate your own with a fine grater.

Nuts
almonds flat, pointy-tipped nuts having a pitted brown shell enclosing a creamy white kernel that is covered by a brown skin. *Blanched almonds* have had their brown skins removed. *Almond meal* is also known as ground almonds; nuts are powdered to a coarse flour texture for use in baking or as a thickening agent. *Slivered almonds* are small pieces cut lengthways.
cashews plump, kidney-shaped, golden-brown nuts having a distinctive sweet, buttery flavour and containing about 48 per cent fat. Because of this high fat content, they should be kept, sealed tightly, under refrigeration to avoid becoming rancid. We use roasted unsalted cashews in this book, unless otherwise stated; they're available from health-food stores and supermarkets. Roasting cashews brings out their intense nutty flavour.
hazelnuts also known as filberts. Plump, grape-size, rich, sweet nut having a brown inedible skin that is removed by rubbing heated nuts together vigorously in a tea-towel. *Hazelnut meal* is made by grounding the hazelnuts into a coarse flour texture for use in baking or as a thickening agent.
macadamias native to Australia; fairly large, slightly soft, buttery rich nut. Used to make oil and macadamia butter; equally good in salads or cakes and pastries; delicious eaten on their own. Should always be stored in the fridge to prevent their high oil content turning them rancid.
pecans a golden-brown, rich, buttery nut.
pine nuts also known as pignoli; not, in fact, a nut but a small, cream-coloured kernel from pine cones.
pistachios delicately flavoured, pale-green nut inside hard off-white shells. To peel, soak shelled nuts in boiling water for about 5 minutes; drain, then pat dry with absorbent paper. Rub skins with cloth to peel.

Oil
cooking spray we use a cholesterol-free cooking spray made from canola oil.
hazelnut pressed from ground hazelnuts. *see also page 8*
macadamia *see page 8*

olive made from ripened olives. Extra virgin and virgin are the first and second press, respectively, and are therefore considered the best; "extra light" or "light" types refers to taste not fat levels. *see also page 8*

peanut pressed from ground peanuts; the most commonly used oil in Asian cooking because of its high smoke point (capacity to handle high heat without burning). *see also page 8*

sesame made from roasted, crushed, white sesame seeds; a flavouring rather than a cooking medium. *see also page 8*

vegetable sourced from plants rather than animal fats. *see also page 8*

walnut pressed from ground walnuts. *see also page 8*

Olives
kalamata small, sharp-tasting brine-cured black olives.

green harvested before fully ripened and are, as a rule, denser and more bitter than their black or brown relatives.

niçoise small black olives.

Onions
brown and white are interchangeable. Their pungent flesh adds flavour to a vast range of dishes.

fried sold in Asian grocery stores packed in jars or in cellophane bags. Make your own by cutting onions into paper-thin slices, then deep-frying in peanut oil; drain on absorbent paper before storing in an airtight container.

green also known as scallion or, incorrectly, shallot; an immature onion picked before the bulb has formed, having a long, bright-green edible stalk.

red also known as spanish, red spanish or bermuda onion; a sweet-flavoured, large, purple-red onion.

shallot also called french or golden shallot or eschalot; small, brown-skinned member of the onion family. Grows in tight clusters similar to garlic.

spring crisp, narrow green-leafed tops and a round sweet white bulb larger than green onions.

Orecchiette pasta small disc-shaped pasta; translates literally as "little ears".

Oregano *see herbs; see also page 10*

Oyster sauce *see sauces*

Pancetta *see pork*

Papaya, green unripe papaya. Available at Asian food stores; look for one that is hard and slightly shiny, proving it is freshly picked. Papaya will soften rapidly if not used within a day or two.

Paprika ground dried sweet red capsicum (bell pepper); there are many grades and types available, including sweet, hot, mild and smoked.

Parmesan *see cheese*

Parsley, flat-leaf *see herbs; see also page 10*

Passionfruit also known as granadilla; a small tropical fruit, comprised of a tough outer skin surrounding edible black sweet-sour seeds.

Pecans *see nuts*

Pecorino cheese *see cheese*

Pepitas dried pumpkin seeds.

Peppercorns
black the berry clusters are plucked when not quite ripe then left to ferment then dry in the sun until they are shrivelled and nearly black.

green soft, unripe berry of the pepper plant; usually sold packed in brine (occasionally found dried, packed in salt). Has a fresher flavour and less pungency than black pepper.

pink not actually a member of the pepper family although it is often marketed as such; is the dried berry from a type of rose plant grown in Madagascar. Usually sold packed in brine; has a pungently sweet taste.

sichuan also known as szechuan or chinese pepper, native to the Sichuan province of China. Small, mildly-hot, red-brown aromatic seeds that resemble

black peppercorns; they have a peppery-lemon flavour. Although it is not related to the peppercorn family, the berries look like black peppercorns.

white from the fully ripened berries that are just about to turn red. After harvest the clusters are soaked in water, which softens the outer coating to reveal grey centres. Once dried, they become naturally bleached to white.

Pepper medley a mixture of black, white, green and pink peppercorns, coriander seeds and allspice; sold in disposable grinders in supermarkets. You can make your own blend using various peppercorns.

Pepperoni a spicy variety of dry salami usually made of pork and beef, although other meats can be used, and heavily seasoned with spices.

Pine nuts *see nuts*

Piri piri sauce *see sauces*

Pistachios *see nuts*

Plum sauce *see sauces*

Polenta also known as cornmeal; a flour-like cereal made of dried corn (maize); sold ground in different textures. Also the name of the dish made from it.

Pomegranate native to the Middle East; a dark-red, leathery-skinned fresh fruit about the size of a large orange. Each fruit is filled with hundreds of seeds, each wrapped in an edible lucent-crimson pulp having a unique tangy sweet-sour flavour.

Poppy seeds
black small, dried, bluish-grey seeds of the poppy plant, with a crunchy texture and a nutty flavour. Can be purchased whole or ground in most supermarkets.

white also known as kas kas. Quite dissimilar to the black variety, these seeds from the white poppy are used, ground, as a thickening agent in sauces or as a substitute for ground almonds.

Pork
belly fatty cut sold in rashers or in a piece, with or without rind or bone.

butterflied steak boneless mid-loin chop, split in half and flattened.

chinese barbecued roasted pork fillet with a sweet, sticky coating. Available from Asian food shops or specialty stores.

cutlet sirloin cutlets are boneless thin cuts of meat from the loin; leg cutlets are cut from the middle of the leg.

fillet boneless eye-fillet cut from the loin. It is one of the most tender cuts of pork.

loin chop tender, prime chops with a characteristic T-bone on one side.

medallions pork fillet sliced crosswise and opened out.

neck sometimes called pork scotch; cut from the foreloin without any bones.

pancetta an Italian unsmoked bacon; pork belly that is cured in salt and spices then rolled into a sausage shape and dried for several weeks.

prosciutto cured, air-dried (unsmoked), pressed ham.

shoulder joint sold with bone in or out.

spareribs long cut from the lower portion of the pig, and includes up to 13 long bones.

Potatoes
baby new also known as chats; not a separate variety but an early harvest with very thin skin.

coliban round, smooth white skin and flesh; good for baking and mashing.

desiree oval, smooth and pink-skinned, waxy yellow flesh; good in salads, boiled and roasted.

kipfler small, finger-shaped potato with a nutty flavour.

nicola medium-sized, oval, beige skin, yellow flesh; good for mashing.

pontiac large, red skin, deep eyes, white flesh; good grated, boiled and baked.

russet burbank also called idaho; long and oval, rough white skin with shallow eyes, white flesh; good for baking and frying.

sebago white skin, oval; good fried, mashed and baked.

spunta large, long, yellow flesh, floury; great mashed and fried.

Poultry

chicken, barbecued a shop-bought whole barbecued chicken weighing about 900g.

chicken breast fillet breast halved, skinned and boned.

chicken drumette small fleshy part of the wing between shoulder and elbow, trimmed to resemble a drumstick.

chicken drumstick leg with skin and bone intact.

chicken maryland leg and thigh still connected in a single piece; bones and skin intact.

chicken, small also known as spatchcock (poussin), no more than 6 weeks old, weighing a maximum of 500g.

chicken thigh skin and thigh bone intact.

chicken thigh fillet thigh with skin and centre bone removed.

chicken wing the whole wing, bone and skin intact.

duck, chinese barbecued traditionally cooked in special ovens in China; dipped into and brushed during roasting with a sticky sweet coating made from soy sauce, sherry, ginger, five-spice, star anise and hoisin sauce. Available from Asian food shops as well as dedicated Chinese barbecued meat shops.

duck maryland thigh and drumstick still connected; skin still on.

quail small, delicate-flavoured game birds ranging in weight from 250g to 300g; also known as partridge.

turkey breast fillet breast halved, skinned and boned.

Preserved lemon a North African specialty; lemons are quartered and preserved in salt, lemon juice and water. To use, remove and discard pulp, squeeze juice from rind; rinse rind well then slice thinly. Sold in jars or singly by delicatessens; once opened, store under refrigeration.

Prosciutto *see pork*

Ras el hanout a classic spice blend used in Moroccan cooking. The name means "top of the shop" and is the very best spice blend that a spice merchant has to offer.

Rice

arborio small, round-grain rice well-suited to absorb a large amount of liquid; the high level of starch makes it especially suitable for risottos.

basmati a white, fragrant, long-grained rice; the grains fluff up beautifully when cooked. It should be washed several times before cooking.

brown is the entire grain with only the inedible outer husk removed. The nutritious, high-fibre bran coating gives it a light tan colour, nut-like flavour and chewy texture.

long-grain elongated grains that remain separate when cooked; this is the most popular steaming rice in Asia.

wild not a true member of the rice family but a very dark brown seed of a North American aquatic grass; has a distinctively nutty flavour and crunchy, resilient texture. Sold on its own or in a blend with basmati or long-grain white rice.

Ricotta *see cheese*

Risoni also known as risi; small, rice-shaped pasta very similar to another small pasta, orzo.

Roquefort *see cheese*

Rosemary pungent herb with long, thin pointy leaves; available fresh or dried. *see also page 11*

Sage pungent herb with narrow, grey-green leaves; slightly bitter with a light musty mint aroma.

Sake Japan's favourite wine; made from fermented rice and used for marinating and cooking. If sake is unavailable, dry sherry, vermouth or brandy can be substituted.

Sambal oelek (also ulek or olek); Indonesian in origin, this is a salty paste made from ground chillies and vinegar.

Sashimi fish sold as sashimi has to meet stringent guidelines regarding its handling. We suggest you seek local advice from authorities before easting any raw seafood.

Savoy cabbage large, heavy head with crinkled dark-green outer leaves; a fairly mild tasting cabbage. *see also page 13*

Sauces

barbecue a spicy, tomato-based sauce used to marinate or baste, or as a condiment.

fish also called nam pla or nuoc nam; made from pulverised salted fermented fish, most often anchovies. Has a pungent smell and strong taste. There are many versions of varying intensity, so use according to your taste.

hoisin a thick, sweet and spicy Chinese paste made from salted fermented soy beans, onions and garlic. Used as a marinade or a baste, or to accent stir-fries.

oyster Asian in origin, this rich, brown sauce is made from oysters and their brine, cooked with salt and soy sauce, and thickened with starches.

piri piri an extremely hot chilli sauce used in Portuguese, African and Brazilian cookery. It is available in bottles from major supermarkets. Also an African word for chilli.

plum a thick, sweet and sour dipping sauce made from plums, vinegar, sugar, chillies and spices.

soy also known as sieu; made from fermented soya beans. There are several variations available in most Asian food stores and supermarkets. We use a mild Japanese variety unless otherwise indicated.

dark soy deep brown, almost black in colour; rich, with a thicker consistency than other types. Pungent but not particularly salty.

japanese soy an all-purpose low-sodium soy sauce made with more wheat content than its Chinese counterparts. Possibly the best table soy and the one to choose if you only want one variety.

kecap manis a dark, thick sweet soy sauce used in most South-East Asian cuisines. The soy's sweetness is derived from the addition of molasses or palm sugar when brewed.

light soy a fairly thin, pale and salty tasting sauce; used in dishes in which the natural colour of the ingredients is to be maintained. Not to be confused with salt-reduced or low-sodium soy sauces.

sweet chilli a mild sauce made from red chillies, sugar, garlic and vinegar.

Tabasco brand name of an extremely fiery sauce made from vinegar, red thai chillies and salt.

teriyaki a Japanese sauce made from soy sauce, mirin, sugar, ginger and other spices; imparts a distinctive glaze when brushed over grilled meat or poultry.

tomato also known as catsup or ketchup; a sauce made from tomatoes, vinegar and spices.

vegetarian mushroom oyster this is a "vegetarian" oyster sauce made from blended mushrooms and soy sauce.

worcestershire a spicy dark-coloured sauce made from garlic, soy sauce, onions, lime, tamarind, molasses, anchovies, vinegar and seasonings. This condiment was invented by the English in India.

Sausages

chipolata also known as "little fingers"; highly spiced, coarse-textured beef sausage.

chorizo Spanish origin; made from coarsely ground pork and highly seasoned with garlic and chillies.

merguez a small, spicy sausage believed to have originated in Tunisia but eaten throughout North Africa, France and Spain. Merguez is traditionally made with lamb and is easily recognised because of its chilli-red colour.

italian a coarse pork sausage, generally sold in plump links. Usually flavoured with garlic and fennel seed or anise seed. It comes as hot (with red thai chilli), and sweet (without the heat). It must be well cooked before serving.

Seafood

balmain bug also known as slipper or shovelnose lobster, or southern bay lobster; is a crustacean, a type of crayfish. Substitute with moreton bay bugs, king prawns or scampi.

barramundi fillet an Aboriginal word meaning "river fish with large scales". A firm, moist white fish.

black mussels should be bought from a fish market where there is reliably fresh fish; must be tightly closed when bought, indicating they are alive. Before cooking, scrub the shells with a strong brush and remove the beards. Discard any shells that do not open after cooking. Varieties also include green-lip.

blue-eye also known as deep sea trevalla or trevally and blue-eye cod; thick, moist white-fleshed fish. Available as cutlets or fillets.

bream (yellowfin) also known as silver or black bream, seabream or surf bream; soft, moist white flesh. Substitute with snapper or ocean perch.

calamari a mollusc (type of squid); can be substituted with baby octopus.

firm white fish fillets blue-eye, bream, flathead, swordfish, ling, whiting, jewfish, snapper or sea perch are all good choices. Check for any small pieces of bone in the fillets and use tweezers to remove them.

garfish small, long, slender fish with a readily distinguished beak-like elongation of the lower jaw. The flesh is sweet with a firm texture, but watch out for the fine bones.

kingfish (yellowtail) also known as southern yellowfish, kingie or tasmanian yellowtail. Substitute with jewfish.

lobster (rock lobster) also known as cray, spiny lobster, eastern, southern or western lobster. Substitute with balmain or moreton bay bugs.

mahi mahi also known as dolphin fish or dorado. Substitute with swordfish, mako shark or striped marlin.

ocean trout a farmed fish with pink, soft flesh. From the same family as the atlantic salmon; one can be substituted for the other.

octopus usually tenderised before you buy them. Both octopus and squid require either long slow cooking or quick cooking over high heat; anything in between will make them tough and rubbery.

oysters varieties include pacific, bay, blacklip, sydney or new zealand rock oyster.

prawns also known as shrimp. Varieties include school, king, royal red, sydney harbour or tiger. Buy uncooked (green) or cooked, with or without shells.

salmon red-pink firm flesh with few bones; has a moist delicate flavour.

sardines also known as pilchards; small silvery fish with soft, oily flesh. Substitute with garfish.

scallops a bivalve mollusc with a fluted shell valve; we use scallops that have the coral (roe) attached.

snapper a saltwater fish; the most popular is red snapper, however, it also includes gray snapper, mutton snapper, schoolmaster snapper and yellowtail snapper. Has a firm textured flesh and very little fat. The smaller sizes are often sold whole, while larger fish can be purchased in steaks and fillets.

squid also known as calamari; a type of mollusc. Buy squid hoods to make preparation and cooking faster.

swordfish also called broadbill. Substitute with yellowfin or bluefin tuna or mahi mahi.

whiting (sand whiting) also called trumpeter, silver whiting, king george whiting or summer whiting. Substitute with bream.

Sesame seeds black and white are the most common of this small oval seed, however, there are also red and brown varieties. To toast: spread seeds evenly on oven tray, toast briefly in a moderate oven.

Shallots *see onion*

Sherry fortified wine consumed as an aperitif or used in cooking. Sold as fino (dry, light), amontillado (medium sweet, dark) and oloroso (full-bodied, very dark).

Silver beet also known as swiss chard and, incorrectly, spinach; has fleshy stalks and large dark-green leaves.

Snow peas also called mange tout (eat all). Snow pea sprouts, the growing shoots of the plant, are sold by greengrocers.

Snow pea tendrils *see page 13*

Soy sauce *see sauces*

Spinach also known as english spinach and incorrectly, silver beet.

Squash, yellow patty-pan also known as crookneck or custard marrow pumpkins; a round, slightly flat summer squash being yellow to pale-green in colour and having a scalloped edge. Harvested young, it has a firm white flesh and a distinct flavour.

Star anise a dried star-shaped fruit of a tree native to China. The pods have an astringent aniseed or licorice flavour. Available whole and ground. It is an essential ingredient in chinese five-spice powder.

Star fruit also known as carambola, five-corner fruit or chinese star fruit; pale green or yellow in colour, it has a clean, crisp texture. Flavour may be either sweet or sour, depending on the variety and when it was picked. There is no need to peel or seed it and they're slow to discolour.

Stock available in cans, bottles or tetra packs. Stock cubes or powder can be used. As a guide, 1 teaspoon of stock powder or 1 small crumbled stock cube mixed with 1 cup (250ml) water will give a fairly strong stock.

Sugar

brown an extremely soft, finely granulated sugar retaining molasses for its characteristic colour and flavour.

caster also known as finely granulated or superfine table sugar.

icing sugar also known as confectioners' sugar or powdered sugar; granulated sugar crushed together with a small amount of cornflour.

icing sugar, pure also known as confectioners' sugar or powdered sugar; has no added cornflour.

palm sugar also known as nam tan pip, jaggery, jawa or gula melaka; made from the sap of the sugar palm tree. Light brown to black in colour and usually sold in rock-hard cakes; the sugar of choice in Indian and most South-East Asian cooking. If unavailable, substitute with brown sugar.

white a coarse, granulated table sugar, also known as crystal sugar.

Sugar snap peas also known as honey snap peas; a fresh small pea that can be eaten whole, pod and all.

Sultanas dried grapes, also known as golden raisins.

Sumac an astringent purple-red spice ground from berries growing on shrubs that flourish wild around the Mediterranean; has a tart, lemony flavour. Available from Middle-Eastern grocery stores and some major supermarkets.

Sunflower seed kernels grey-green, slightly soft, kernels.

Tabasco sauce *see sauces*

Tabbouleh a Middle-eastern dish made with bulgur wheat, tomatoes, onions, parsley, mint, olive oil and lemon juice.

Taco seasoning mix found in most supermarkets; is meant to duplicate the taste of a Mexican sauce made from oregano, cumin, chillies and other spices.

Tahini a rich sesame-seed paste available from Middle-Eastern grocery stores and health-food shops; often used in hummus, baba ghanoush and other Lebanese recipes.

Tamarind concentrate the commercial distillation of tamarind pulp into a condensed paste. Thick and purple-black, it is ready-to-use, with no soaking or straining required; can be diluted with water according to taste. Found in Asian supermarkets.

Tarragon see herbs; see also page 11

Teriyaki sauce see sauces

Thyme see herbs; see also page 11

Tofu also known as bean curd; an off-white, custard-like product made from the "milk" of crushed soya beans. Comes fresh as soft or firm, and processed as fried or pressed dried sheets. Leftover fresh tofu can be refrigerated in water (which is changed daily) for up to four days.

Tomatoes
cherry also known as tiny tim or tom thumb tomatoes; small, round tomatoes.
egg also called plum or roma, these are smallish, oval-shaped tomatoes.
grape small, long oval-shaped tomatoes with a good flavour.
pasta sauce a prepared tomato-based sauce (sometimes called ragu or sugo on the label); comes in varying degrees of thickness and with different flavourings.
paste triple-concentrated tomato puree.
semi-dried partially dried tomato pieces in olive oil; softer and juicier than sun-dried, these are not preserved thus do not keep as long as sun-dried.
sun-dried in oil tomato pieces that have been dried with salt; this dehydrates the tomato and concentrates the flavour. We use sun-dried tomatoes packaged in oil, unless otherwise specified.
sun-dried tomato pesto a thick paste made from sun-dried tomatoes, oil, vinegar and herbs.
truss also known as vine-ripened tomatoes. Small vine-ripened tomatoes with the vine still attached.

Turmeric available fresh and ground. Fresh is also known as kamin; is a rhizome related to galangal and ginger. Must be grated or pounded to release its somewhat acrid aroma and pungent flavour.

Vanilla
bean dried, long, thin pod from a tropical golden orchid; the minuscule black seeds inside the bean are used to impart a luscious vanilla flavour in baking and desserts. Place a whole bean in a jar of sugar to make the vanilla sugar often called for in recipes; a bean can be used three or four times.
extract obtained from vanilla beans infused in water.

Veal
cutlets a small cut of meat, usually from the leg or ribs.
loin chops cut from the loin section.
fillet also known as tenderloin; a long, boneless cut of meat from the loin.

Vegetarian mushroom oyster sauce see sauces

Vietnamese mint see herbs; see also page 10

Vinegar
balsamic there are many balsamic vinegars on the market ranging in pungency and quality depending on how, and for how long, they have been aged. It is a deep rich brown colour with a sweet and sour flavour. Quality can be determined up to a point by price; use the most expensive sparingly. see also page 9
cider also known as apple cider vinegar; made from fermented apples. see also page 9
malt made from fermented malt and beech shavings. see also page 9
raspberry made from fresh raspberries steeped in a white wine vinegar.
red wine made from red wine. see also page 9
rice a colourless vinegar made from fermented rice and flavoured with sugar and salt. Also known as seasoned rice vinegar; sherry can be substituted. see also page 9
sherry natural vinegar aged in oak according to the traditional Spanish system; a mellow wine vinegar named for its colour. see also page 9
white made from spirit of cane sugar.
white wine made from white wine. see also page 9

Walnuts see nuts

Wasabi a pungent, green-coloured horseradish accompaniment; sold in powdered or paste form.

Water chestnut resemble true chestnuts in appearance, hence the English name. Small brown tubers with a crisp, white, nutty-tasting flesh. Best experienced fresh; however, canned water chestnuts are more easily obtained and can be kept for about a month in the refrigerator, once opened.

Watercress one of the cress family, a large group of peppery greens. Highly perishable, so it must be used as soon as possible after purchase. see also page 13

Wombok also known as peking cabbage, chinese cabbage or petsai. Elongated in shape with pale green, crinkly leaves, this is the most common cabbage in South-East Asian cooking.

Wonton wrappers and gow gee or spring roll pastry sheets, made of flour, egg and water, are found in the refrigerated or freezer section of Asian food shops and many supermarkets. These come in different thicknesses and shapes. Thin wrappers work best in soups, while the thicker ones are best for frying; and the choice of round or square, small or large is dependent on the recipe.

Worcestershire sauce see sauces

Yeast (dried and fresh), a raising agent used in dough making. A microscopic living organism that grows best in warm, moist conditions; over-hot conditions or dissolving liquid will kill yeast and keep the dough from rising. Granular (7g sachets) and fresh compressed (20g blocks) yeast can almost always be substituted one for the other when yeast is called for.

Yogurt we use plain full-cream yogurt in our recipes unless specifically noted otherwise. If a recipe in this book calls for low-fat yogurt, we use one with a fat content of less than 0.2 per cent.

Za'atar a blend of whole roasted sesame seeds, sumac and crushed dried herbs. Available from spice shops and Middle-Eastern food stores.

Zucchini also known as courgette; small, pale- or dark-green, yellow or white vegetable belonging to the squash family. Its young flowers are also edible.

conversion chart

MEASURES

One Australian metric measuring cup holds approximately 250ml; one Australian metric tablespoon holds 20ml; one Australian metric teaspoon holds 5ml.

The difference between one country's measuring cups and another's is within a two- or three-teaspoon variance, and will not affect your cooking results. North America, New Zealand and the United Kingdom use a 15ml tablespoon.

All cup and spoon measurements are level. The most accurate way of measuring dry ingredients is to weigh them. When measuring liquids, use a clear glass or plastic jug with the metric markings.

We use large eggs with an average weight of 60g.

DRY MEASURES

metric	imperial
15g	½oz
30g	1oz
60g	2oz
90g	3oz
125g	4oz (¼lb)
155g	5oz
185g	6oz
220g	7oz
250g	8oz (½lb)
280g	9oz
315g	10oz
345g	11oz
375g	12oz (¾lb)
410g	13oz
440g	14oz
470g	15oz
500g	16oz (1lb)
750g	24oz (1½lb)
1kg	32oz (2lb)

LIQUID MEASURES

metric	imperial
30ml	1 fluid oz
60ml	2 fluid oz
100ml	3 fluid oz
125ml	4 fluid oz
150ml	5 fluid oz (¼ pint/1 gill)
190ml	6 fluid oz
250ml	8 fluid oz
300ml	10 fluid oz (½ pint)
500ml	16 fluid oz
600ml	20 fluid oz (1 pint)
1000ml (1 litre)	1¾ pints

LENGTH MEASURES

metric	imperial
3mm	⅛in
6mm	¼in
1cm	½in
2cm	¾in
2.5cm	1in
5cm	2in
6cm	2½in
8cm	3in
10cm	4in
13cm	5in
15cm	6in
18cm	7in
20cm	8in
23cm	9in
25cm	10in
28cm	11in
30cm	12in (1ft)

OVEN TEMPERATURES

These oven temperatures are only a guide for conventional ovens. For fan-forced ovens, check the manufacturer's manual.

	°C (Celsius)	°F (Fahrenheit)	Gas Mark
Very slow	120	250	½
Slow	150	275-300	1-2
Moderately slow	160	325	3
Moderate	180	350-375	4-5
Moderately hot	200	400	6
Hot	220	425-450	7-8
Very hot	240	475	9

index

General manager *Christine Whiston*
Editor-in-Chief *Susan Tomnay*
Creative director *Hieu Chi Nguyen*
Designer *Clare O'Loughlin*
Senior editor *Stephanie Kistner*
Food writer *Xanthe Roberts*
Food director *Pamela Clark*
Food editor *Cathie Lonnie*

Sales & rights director *Brian Cearnes*
Marketing manager *Bridget Cody*
Senior business analyst *Rebecca Varela*
Circulation manager *Jarna Mclean*
Operations manager *David Scotto*
Production manager *Victoria Jefferys*

ACP Books are published by ACP Magazines
a division of PBL Media Pty Limited
PBL Media, Chief Executive Officer *Ian Law*
Publishing & sales director, Women's lifestyle *Lynette Phillips*
Group editorial director, Women's lifestyle *Pat Ingram*
Marketing director, Women's lifestyle *Matthew Dominello*
Commercial manager, Women's lifestyle *Seymour Cohen*
Research Director, Women's lifestyle *Justin Stone*

Cover photographer *Dean Wilmot*
Cover stylist *Sarah De Nardi*
Cover photochef *Kirrily La Rosa*

Special feature photographers *Vanessa Levis, Stuart Scott*
Special feature stylist *Sarah De Nardi*
Special feature photochefs *Dominique Gekas,
Rebecca Squadrito*

Produced by ACP Books, Sydney.
Published by ACP Books, a division of ACP Magazines Ltd.
54 Park St, Sydney NSW Australia 2000. GPO Box 4088, Sydney, NSW 2001.
Phone +61 2 9282 8618 Fax +61 2 9267 9438
acpbooks@acpmagazines.com.au www.acpbooks.com.au
Printed by Toppan Printing Co., in China.

Australia Distributed by Network Services, GPO Box 4088, Sydney, NSW 2001.
Phone +61 2 9282 8777 Fax +61 2 9264 3278
networkweb@networkservicescompany.com.au
United Kingdom Distributed by Australian Consolidated Press (UK),
10 Scirocco Close, Moulton Park Office Village, Northampton, NN3 6AP.
Phone +44 1604 642 200 Fax +44 1604 642 300
books@acpuk.com www.acpuk.com
New Zealand Distributed by Southern Publishers Group, 21 Newton Road, Auckland.
Phone +64 9 360 0692 Fax +64 9 360 0695 hub@spg.co.nz
South Africa Distributed by PSD Promotions, 30 Diesel Road Isando, Gauteng
Johannesburg. PO Box 1175, Isando 1600, Gauteng Johannesburg.
Phone +27 11 392 6065/6/7 Fax +27 11 392 6079/80 orders@psdprom.co.za
Canada Distributed by Publishers Group Canada
Order Desk & Customer Service 9050 Shaughnessy Street, Vancouver, BC V6P 6E5
Phone (800) 663 5714 Fax (800) 565 3770 service@raincoast.com

Title: Salad / Compiler: Pamela Clark.
ISBN: 978-1-86396-875-1 (pbk)
Notes: Includes index.
Subjects: Salads.
Other Authors/Contributors: Clark, Pamela
Dewey Number: 641.83

© ACP Magazines Ltd 2009
ABN 18 053 273 546

This publication is copyright. No part of it may be reproduced or transmitted
in any form without the written permission of the publishers.

To order books, phone 136 116 (within Australia) or online at www.acpbooks.com.au
Send recipe enquiries to: recipeenquiries@acpmagazines.com.au